GOOD COURAGE

INSPIRATION FOR THE EVENING OF LIFE

Thomas van der Horst

Gozalov Books
The Hague

By Thomas van der Horst
Editor: Joya Stevenson
Translator: Guram Kochi MSc

© Thomas van der Horst & Gozalov Books,
The Hague, 2025
Tel.: +31 (0)6 149 88 056
E-mail: g.kochi27@gmail.com
Website: www.hetsmallepad.nl

ISBN: 9789079889846; 978-90-79889-84-6

Unless otherwise indicated, all biblical texts are cited from the NRSV Catholic Edition.

New Revised Standard Version Bible: Catholic Edition, copyright © 1989, 1993 the Division of Christian Education of the National Council of the Churches of Christ in the United States of America. Used by permission. All rights reserved.

Illustrations: Thomas van der Horst

All rights reserved. No part of this publication may be reproduced and/or published by means of printing, photocopying, microfilm or in any other way stored in an automated database without the prior written permission of the publisher.

Contents

Foreword by the author 5

The sun rises happily! 8

Autumn in life 11

Being old means 13

Advent Quartet: Four weeks
on the way to Christmas 22

The Christmas Story: An Invitation to Us All 33

Angels 40

Walking and wondering 45

Conserving and Preserving 47

Psalm 121 55

Experiencing loss 56

Ascending to the Light 63

Prayer for a blessed death 72

Pain 74

Flowers and those who love them 80

Loneliness 85

What do you live for? 91

Spring, Lent and Easter 95

Wind – Water – Light	102
'Our mother'	105
Was everything created?	112
Mary, the Mother of the Lord	122
The Hail Mary	130
Pentecost: Baptized in Fire	133
Pigeon story 1	149
Your soul	152
Finding a foothold in prayer	154
Remembering and commemorating	164
Sacred by nature	168
Redemption	174
Gifts for the Redeemer.	
Christmas meditation	176
The King's Children	182
New Year's Eve news	187
That one day	190
Love as the fullness of life	193
Thou	196

Foreword by the author

Could it be that deep inside every person a small pilot light is burning? Spirituality generally has to do with life questions. You will find a variety of subjects in this book, which can stand on their own and be read separately.

The order followed in this book is more or less that of the church year, which partly overlaps the calendar year, from the end of November to the end of November in consecutive years. The book has separate thematic sections. If you wish, you can browse through them at random.

The book title Good Courage is inspired by the Limburg wish for a prosperous New Year: 'Goeie roetsj', they say in Limburg on December 31. With that wish in mind, Good Courage sounds clear and uplifting. "Yes, we need that these days," I hear many people say.

Many elderly people enjoy reading. At an older age, however, reading does not always go as smoothly as it used to. Technical difficulties may arise in reading small print within long blocks of text.

In addition, there is little reading material available explicitly for elderly people as a target group. That is a loss. Hence this book, which has been extensively read, considered, and evaluated by elderly people in Heerlen. My late father, who lived in The Hague, was himself, at his advanced age, a critical and expert reader. I owe him a lot.
This book regularly quotes the Bible. Hopefully, that won't put you off if you're not used to dealing with the Bible.

It is the living God Who speaks to you when you open the Bible. So, you never read the Bible alone, but always together with our God, the Living Word Himself! To read the Bible is like taking a walk with God in order to get to know each other.

My first writings appeared at the beginning of the corona virus period in March 2020. Quite a lot of writing followed after that. And in this volume, you will find a number of my writings edited and bundled, with great thanks to family and friends who have read previous versions carefully.

I wish you much joy and inspiration while reading.

Thomas van der Horst

About the Author

Thomas van der Horst is a Roman-Catholic theologian and spiritual counselor (retired Januari 2025) in Heerlen, Netherlands. He completed his full training at the Major Seminary Rolduc in Kerkrade, Netherlands, and a doctorate at the Catholic Theological University Utrecht-Amsterdam. Van der Horst has obtained specialized training in spiritual care for the elderly. This training includes the following professional certificates: the Elderly Care (NCOI) Certificate, the Certificate of Elderly Advisor (Christian University of Applied Sciences, Ede, Netherlands), and the Certificate of Discussion Leader in Moral Consultation (Utrecht University, Netherlands). Van der Horst has also studied intensively at the Study House of the Church Fathers

(Gent, Belgium). His publications include a translation of various texts, by and about the orthodox theologian Alexander Schmemann, entitled *The Holy Week in Orthodoxy*. A liturgical explanation of the Holy Week, published in 2023 by Gozalov Books, The Hague. Van der Horst, who is not an ordained priest, is married with two children.

The sun rises happily!

The sun rises radiantly, every new day, at least that is how people experience it. In fact, the sun never rises or sets, it has been shining continuously for billions of years. As soon as the sun appears, a feeling of joy arises.

In the evening, we can trust that the sun will continue to shine behind the horizon while we sleep. And just when we have had enough rest, the sun appears again. Its light wakes us up and brings us to life. This daily pattern, this masterful attunement, has something wonderful about it.

Those who wake up just before sunrise taste the silence of the early morning, and they have time to wonder, again, what day it is. Some even reflect that this new day is a gift from God. So, it is time for the first prayer: "Sweet Lord, thank you for this wonderful day," prays a 102-year-old who learned this prayer from her mother. At this moment, there comes a certainty of divine joy, for you know that God is present in every beginning and lets His loving light shine. The miracle is too great for the human heart. Human beings hope that this new day, once again, will offer unsuspected openings. After all, every day begins new.

And just as every new day has never existed before, so every person is a new beginning. Every person is unique, having been given a proper name, just as every day has its own date. That makes the new day special. Every person may and can rejoice in it. With every new day, you add a new piece to the long history of God's dealings with man.

In this way, we help building His Kingdom. From that awareness comes a cheerful mood in the heart and an immense joy at the start of the day! Indeed, every day begins as a miracle. The sun that rises is a creature just as we are. Certainly, the sun is a great and radiant symbol of the Creator Who created heaven and earth. And yet, the sun is not the most perfect and greatest symbol of God. Though it radiates light, it cannot radiate love. There is another symbol of God's Love that is even greater and more radiant than the sun, namely the human being. The human is called to radiate God's Love from his own free choice. To be of value as a human being to my fellows means to let the Invisible Sun, Who is God, rise in the life of my neighbor.

No human being will live a day without the light of this Invisible Sun! To give light and love can be done in so many different ways: listening, being attentive, helping, or offering a joint prayer. Especially do all with humor, with a grain of salt that makes the heavy heart a little lighter. And the day becomes a little more bearable for those who find life to be unendurable.

Prayer in the silence of the early morning is like the song of the blackbird, perhaps even the crowing of the rooster, the call to Our Father in heaven. The first contact after waking up is like a "Good morning," because that is what God and man, so to speak, say to each other: "I am here for you and with you today!"

Autumn in life

In autumn, the colors seem to celebrate the passing away of life. As if there is nothing to be sad about. Or do the autumn leaves themselves mourn the short life that has been given to them? Have they perhaps put on their most colorful coats, knowing that their task is complete? They have served the tree, promoted its growth. Would the tree in turn say goodbye, with a heavy heart, to its leaves, which were so kind, which not only gave nourishment, but also splendor and beauty?

The branches and leaves have welcomed many guests since early spring: birds that built their nests, while whistling, and sheltered their little ones. The branches support the young as they grow big and fly away. They hear the daily concert of the songbirds with their song of songs, but perhaps also the noise of the traffic below and of squirrels jumping from branch to branch. The acorns and chestnuts fall first and then the leaves. And the branches and the tree itself may fear the autumn storms.

For centuries, trees could withstand the elements until a gust of wind, a fire, or a person with a saw determined their fate. Whatever the case, the days of every tree are numbered. Whether you are a believer or not, this is the hard law of every life and therefore also of human life.

Apparently, the vulnerability and fragility of all that is temporary is a characteristic of earthly life. This vulnerable tenderness raises the question of the meaning of life as a whole. What is it all about? People can put the question off for their whole life long. As we grow older, the moment inevitably comes when we must pose this question to ourselves.

It could, just as well, be the question of a friend who visits you for a pleasant and personal conversation: "What is important to you today?"

Being old means

"Getting old is nice, but being old is different," we hear each other say so often. We know all too well what is meant. It therefore seems superfluous to stop and think about it. Should we try now? What does it mean to be old? It is a question that must be raised again and again. There are many possible answers and everyone has his or her own thoughts and feelings. At the same time, there are continuous themes and parallel experiences that we share with one another.
Here is a list of some of them.

retirement

There are people who retire at the age of 55 but who feel anything but old. They can still take on the whole world. There are even people who happily continue to work until they are 80, professionally or as a volunteer. They do not feel old at all in the sense of being deficient.

The majority of people look forward to retirement. For example, raising the retirement age for the current sixty-somethings is quite a challenge. Now that I am getting a few grey hairs myself, someone recently said to me: "Do you know yet what you are going to do when the time comes?"

Perhaps you can still remember that moment. For many, the day of retirement is etched in their memory. At least as a milestone in their life.

having more time

Time is a somewhat fluid concept: what lasts far too long, for one person, may not last long enough for another. For one, having more time is perfect and long-awaited, and for another, it is a nightmare, like 'suddenly I bump into myself'.

There's a need to find new meanings and set new priorities. Within a marriage, the spouses will come up with new agreements and express their expectations, with regard to each other and to third parties. How are we going to use our time? On top of that, there's a mixture of new feelings, such as that of having been written-off by society, or of no longer being acknowledged. One may miss previous conversation partners. Filling in time is like filling a treasure chest: what is still precious to me and what is not? May every choice certainly be very positive, then!

doing nice things

It seems like a carefree dream. To have all the time in the world to spend: travelling far or walking nearby, getting started with hobbies, making music or going dancing, reading or writing memoirs. There may be a much-needed catch-up with photo albums, looking after grandchildren, maintaining the garden, painting and renovating the house, at last installing a new kitchen, renovating the bathroom, and so on.
Above all, there are no more obligations, at least not such heavy ones, no more daily traffic jams, no sleepless nights, no deadlines, no endless meetings, no more difficult customers, no more incessant phone calls, no more hassle, no more having to get up before dawn.

We accept the inconveniences. "It's not always roses." Our main theme is to enjoy life, because "You only live once!" There's an often-heard sigh, "I've never been busier than since I retired."

becoming less vital

Most mortals, around the age of 60, will start to feel that they are 'no longer 18'— unfortunately. To walk up and down stairs takes a bit more energy and to remember names is no longer as easy. Glasses make their appearance, medication becomes a daily ritual. Those who reach a certain advanced age may describe themselves as extremely vital, and feel that way, but they nevertheless notice that their peers are increasingly dropping off, like leaves falling off the tree of life. Life, which once seemed eternal, presents itself in all its temporality and finiteness. It is starting to creak and groan a bit for most people. You hardly dare to look in the mirror anymore: yet another wrinkle appears on a daily basis. This disaster can be postponed for a while with remedies, but there is no escape, sadly. Hair and teeth fall out here and there. Some proudly tap their heads and cry out, with dread and trembling, "As long as things continue to go well here," and hope that the 'dicky ticker' does not give out. All sorts of things happen that we do not want. "It will have to do!" sounds like a widely spread famous quote. The ravages of time worm and gnaw and make most people creak and groan.

receiving help

An elder recently said: "I would like so much to help other people, but I have the strength to do so no longer. Instead, I myself have to constantly ask for help. " To which I replied: "Can't you, with your will to help others, help your care providers to help you? Receiving help is a true art of living!"

Receiving the goodness of others can be very difficult and hard. It is a skill that seems easy at first glance, but which nevertheless is not self-evident. When you were young, you were allowed to learn by trial and error, but at old age, people prefer not to take that too literally. Then just ask for help more often.

You sometimes hear others sigh: "I find the constant dependency and loss of control the most difficult issue." That is indeed very difficult.
Some people even take it a step further by feeling guilty when asking for help. After all, it wasn't that long ago that you were active yourself and helped others when necessary. However, no one needs to

feel guilty. It is wise to ask for help. Let someone come at the right time.

Thinking differently and no longer feeling guilty: it takes time, but it is more than worth doing for your well-being and your happiness. Being human becomes beautiful and joyful. In giving and receiving help, helper and recipient are there for each other, in equal measure, in a human encounter. Love colors and strengthens our humanity.

detaching

Detachment, though a somewhat old-fashioned concept, is still very meaningful; we are called not to cling so terribly to everything. That is certainly easier said than done and felt.

When people are attached to each other for decades, they have become inwardly one. After a lifetime together, elderly people are sometimes separated overnight, while they had not given it a second thought beforehand. Your partner becomes ill or dies and suddenly you find yourself in a completely different reality.

The loss of a loved one is a forced process of detachment and grieving. The grieving process is further intensified, if additionally, there is a forced move, and one has not even had the chance to say goodbye to their familiar house. To get used to a new living environment can then be experienced, naturally, as a false start. The feeling of home is very far away. Someone is displaced to the depths of their soul. In this way, people can experience an awful lot of stress in the space of just a year.

The only real support, it seems, is provided by close family members and friends who regularly come to visit. These are people with whom you used to share life so pleasantly. How moving it is to experience the contribution our visits make to the lives of our loved ones. The message tells of companionship: "I am still here and you are still here, we are together!"

Detachment and mourning, experiences familiar in the lives of the elderly, can initially deprive people of all their energy. They often feel punished. "I don't know what I have done wrong that this has happened to me!" This is an understandable reaction.

Inherent in our lives is that moment of decline and deterioration that normally comes with age. Jesus made a pertinent statement about this condition, after He had risen and warned His disciples that the end of their lives would bring trials:

> Very truly, I tell you, when you were younger, you used to fasten your own belt and to go wherever you wished. But when you grow old, you will stretch out your hands, and someone else will fasten a belt around you and take you where you do not wish to go.
> John 21:18

Nowadays, we often talk about letting go. It is advisable no longer to cling to what's around you; indeed, it turns out, that you are the one who suffers the most by clinging. Detachment (i.e. to stop clinging) takes time. If approached consciously, with awareness, the process brings healing, eventually. Detachment and letting go usually involve difficult choices. It is like peeling an orange: whoever wants to eat will choose to peel it. That beautiful orange peel is the familiar exterior of things. That's the only coat that you take off during a visit. What remains is the core, the encounter, the life that is tasted. Sure, a new situation—and setting for your life—takes some getting used to, but it will be fine! Trust.

remembering and commemorating

Growing older has to do, still more, with remembering and commemorating—by which we turn the past into the present. We do not want to forget who and what remain dear to us. By remembering another, respectfully, that person remains a fixed point of support in our life. Memory is our soul, the core of our existence.

In the church context, especially at the beginning of November, we explicitly commemorate those who have passed away during the past year. We mention their names on All Souls Day (2 November), and in the liturgy, we also address God in particular: "Remember the names, Lord." That liturgy comforts us greatly, at least if we can go along with the ritual. We wish only that the names and memories of our loved ones shall not be lost.

For relatives, this commemoration may provide a feeling of lasting companionship, as if we are permanently accompanied by our departed loved ones. My father (1926-2024) added this line to the commemorative prayer: "In my youth, gatherings of all kinds - church and non-church - were invariably concluded with the prayer: 'that the souls of the faithful who have passed away may rest in peace through the mercy of God'."

taking stock

To stay with my father's inspiration for a moment, after reading my article about growing old, he noted the following: "An important aspect is missing. The person who is approaching the end of his life is, at some point, besieged by the question of its measure and value. People try to escape this by evading disturbing judgments. But those who do not do face the balancing scales soon reach a critical moment when they have to pray in desperation: "Be pleased, O God, to deliver me" (Psalm 70:1).

This is certainly an important point, but—I notice every day—there are very different opinions about how to come to peace with one's life.

For the time being, it is to be hoped that older people will find the opportunity to discuss this with each other.

being free within

Despite all that you experience in your old age, the limitations you confront, there remains a core of freedom, a heart with desires, a free space to make choices. We call that our 'self', and being yourself', the unique center of our entire person. It is there where we are completely free.

staying joyful

In being able to be oneself lies:

> a source of joy
> a wealth of gifts
> untapped talents
> knowing what your potential still holds
> trusting that things will turn out well
> forgiving others, because no person is perfect
> trusting in one's own abilities
> believing in power from above
> hoping for a miracle
> counting on sunshine, which always comes after rain
> expecting the unexpected
> hiding in the mystery of life
> paying attention to others
> rising even above yourself
> embracing the good
> willing to be positive
> the humor to put things into perspective when you are having a bad day
> the courage to ask for help without feeling guilty
> the hope that looks forward to what is to come
> reflection about your life's destination

> additional concerns beyond those mentioned here

In short:

Being old means so much.
Human beings encounter their deepest core, who they really are in their fragile vulnerability.

Advent Quartet: Four weeks on the way to Christmas

Can you remember that in the past, after Sinterklaas, there were three relatively quiet weeks in December during which Advent was celebrated, as a sober and modest preparation for Christmas? No one would even think of putting a Christmas tree in the living room right after Sinterklaas. That poor thing would have lost all its needles long before Christmas. It was only just before Christmas that a decorated tree appeared in the living room; in the old days, complete with real candles!

Advent is a time of silent waiting, of modest anticipation, of hopeful expectation like that of an expectant mother. "He is coming, He is coming," the Coming One, whose arrival was predicted centuries ago. And while the childlike joy with Sinterklaas has been great, a few weeks later, we have even more reason to be happy and joyful.

Every year, millions of people all over the world celebrate Christmas as the family celebration of the year. The assumption is that at Christmas no one should be alone. Christmas seems like the celebration of being human. That, indeed, touches on the theme of Christmas, which, after all, celebrates the day when God became human in Jesus.

Every Advent Sunday, an extra candle is lit on the Advent wreath. As for turning on the light: strictly speaking, we humans do not actually do that. Nor in the early morning, at the end of each night, does a person, somewhere, switch on the daylight. The Advent wreath is the symbol of light that is offered to us as heavenly light, a marker of a stage on the road to Christmas.

Advent 1. Arrival

Advent is the time when the divine Light comes to us, just as the sun rises, making it lighter in the morning. In the same way, the light rises in our hearts, and thus, Christmas is above all the celebration of God Who wants to take the human being into the light of His Glory, His Lordship. With the birth of Jesus, God moves even more emphatically towards us than He does with the creation of heaven and earth or with every new human child. How do we know this for sure? John the Baptist, the forerunner of Jesus, sends his disciples to Jesus with this question to obtain certainty from Him:

> Are you the one who is to come, or are we to wait for another? Luke 7:19

Expecting the Coming One: that is, Advent, an arrival or 'coming to'.

Here's a little anecdote. Once, as a young priest student, I was in a meeting with clergy from other parishes. An old pastor told me with a distraught face that his rectory had been broken into during the night. Everything downstairs had been turned upside down and valuables stolen. All the pastors in attendance were mourning with him. "But pastor," I said, still a young lad, "Hasn't the Lord said that He will come like a thief in the night? If there is another break-in, you must go straight to the burglar and ask him: Are you the Coming One or should we expect someone else?" But this kind of know-it-all talk did not cheer up the pastor at all. Well, I was still an inexperienced brat in those days.

Advent 2. Through Darkness into Light

The word 'advent' is derived from the Latin 'adventus', which means 'arrival'. No, it is not about the arrival of extra weight, which may be the case after all kinds of caramelized biscuits and marzipan. In the four weeks before Christmas, during the season of Advent, we set out from our own darkness, as it were, to arrive at the Christ child.

Note that we are simultaneously moving towards the shortest and darkest days of the year in nature. Every Advent Sunday, we light a new candle on the Advent wreath. We need more and more light in the darkest days. After all, the days are getting shorter;

it is getting colder and darker. That can increase our feelings of depression.

Yet, we must be attentive to the dark days, and aware of our experiences, just as we reflect deeply upon our loneliness of mind and heart. So, we experience our inner darkness. Attention suggests 'departing from yourself': to experience your lonely situation or aloneness. At the same time, you are 'coming back to yourself' including the bright spots and sunny sides. By being attentive, we restore our balance of mind.

By the way, you do not have to be ashamed of loneliness. In a sense, this loneliness (or aloneness) is part of old age. Most people suffer from it sooner or later. Consider the fact that many loved ones, in your circle, have died before you. Your life may become an uninhabited island, increasingly, where you are left alone. In the late evening of life, we walk, as it were, in a dark forest in which we wish not to get lost. Together, let us pay close attention, hoping for a bright space somewhere in the distance.

The Prophet Isaiah offers encouraging words in one of the Christmas Eve readings:

> 2 The people who walked in darkness
>   have seen a great light;
> those who lived in a land of deep darkness—
>   on them light has shined.
> 3 You have multiplied the nation,
>   you have increased its joy;
> they rejoice before you
>   as with joy at the harvest,
>   as people exult when dividing plunder.
> 4 For the yoke of their burden,
>   and the bar across their shoulders,
>   the rod of their oppressor,
>   you have broken as on the day of Midian.
> 5 For all the boots of the tramping warriors

> and all the garments rolled in blood
> shall be burned as fuel for the fire.
> 6 For a child has been born for us,
> a son given to us;
> authority rests upon his shoulders;
> and he is named
> Wonderful Counselor, Mighty God,
> Everlasting Father, Prince of Peace.
> Isaiah 9:2-6

Isaiah says that our murky life feels like a slave existence, but the divine light that shines in the distance frees us from all despondency. After all, we are meant and created to be free and to live from and for inner contentment. We are destined for a joyful life. Joy goes a little deeper than happiness, which can only be observed from the outside. Joy is rooted deep in our hearts, opening with our entire being to God like a blossoming flower. This "blossoming," a striking word, open the shutters of your soul! Don't hide any longer.

Life in and with God is neither black nor white. God, who sees in secret (Matt 6:4), as Jesus says, is present in a dark heart, which is initially afraid of the light. Moreover, Jesus says, "those who do what is true come to the light" (John 3:21). It often costs us a lot of energy to bring to light thoughts and feelings that we have anxiously hidden for years. That is the beauty of daring to believe. The Bible is clear about this message. Come out of your dark grave, come out, you are a beautiful person, worthy of being seen and heard, your eyes will quickly grow accustomed to the light. Come with us to the shining Christmas child.

Advent 3. The joyful encounter

Just as the seed of a sunflower wants to be planted in a sun-lit place, so is the human being like a sunflower seed too, which can come to full bloom in a place where the Divine Light will shine. The flower that comes out is called joy. That is why the Prophet Isaiah, as quoted above, said: "They will rejoice before you." The phrase "before you" indicates an encounter. A joyful encounter in and with the Light, which is God. After finally arriving, you experience a look, a beholding, as people used to say—yea, even a blessed beholding.

We are on our way to the feast of Light. But in order to see that Divine Light even better at Christmas, there is the loving hand of someone in the darkness, within our lonely minds, Who says to us: "Come, let Me lead you. Don't be afraid. It will be fine. Together we will arrive in Bethlehem."
The name Beth Lehem, from the Hebrew, means house of bread, where our spiritual hunger will ultimately be satisfied, because He Who later declares "I am the Living Bread" will be born there. Of all places!

Christmas relates to our entire humanity in a deeper sense. After all, at Christmas we celebrate that God becomes man. God involves the human being in His own divine intimacy. He removes the loneliness of the first man Adam, that is, the human being. God wants to meet the human, to deliver him from evil. Unimaginable. Indeed, He does that as a small newborn child. The phrase "before you" suddenly sounds very different. This creates a completely new vision of humanity, both in a broad and in a deeper sense. Humanity as God originally intended it in the story of creation is now finally coming into focus and to its full potential!

However precious the birth of a child, Christmas is infinitely more so. Christmas is about the birth of the Son of Man, who will ultimately redeem all of humanity, after 33 years during which he was defeating the devil, undoing his destructive works, sin and death. Jesus spoke regularly about Satan. The devil is a core element in His message.

In our times, moreover, the power of evil cannot be denied. But Christmas impresses upon us that every person who is of good will has the prospect of living as a child of God, before His Face in heavenly paradise for all eternity.

Advent 4. The Biblical spectrum from Adam to Pentecost

At Christmas, the broad spectrum of the Bible becomes visible. On the one side, there's a lonely first man, the 'old' Adam, who receives a fellow human being as a helper from God. His loneliness is reflected in Joseph, who initially doesn't know what to do with the fact of Mary's pregnancy. And on the other side of the Biblical spectrum, there's Jesus as the 'new' Adam, who prays to the Father for a Helper and a Comforter who suits us, namely the Holy Spirit.

God saw the first man, and He saw that it would be "not good" for the human to be alone and God decided to make a suitable helper for him. Only after the creation of all the animals did God put Adam to sleep, into a deep sleep. Under anesthesia, we would say now. And He "took one of his ribs, and he completed it with flesh for it," as "a helper similar to himself," a human being like Adam, and therefore no longer an animal, even though animals can be such easy-going housemates.

The new creature is not entirely identical to Adam: the second human being is a woman, and with that, she is also a first human being, namely the first woman, Eve, the mother of the living. You wouldn't say it, but we experience this story every year anew at Christmas, when we celebrate that the new human being is born in Jesus. God Himself now crawls into the skin of the hum: God becomes human with, or among, people. That is why Jesus also calls Himself the Son of Man.
Oh yes, this certainly remains a remarkable thought: the Creator becomes like a creature, because that is what the Christian faith says. This was predicted very concretely by Isaiah, the prophet, hundreds of years before Jesus' birth with the words:

> For a child has been born for us, a son given to us. Isaiah 9:6

Jesus is announced as our child and our son. Loneliness is over. In the light of Jesus' birth, at Christmas, we are now community: God with all of us, and, in that vein, we with each other.
The term 'God-with-us' used to be so beautifully written on the edge of the guilder. The feast of Christmas, the feast of God's Incarnation, we find on one side of the biblical spectrum, and the feast of Pentecost on the other side.
To look forward to Pentecost is to look forward to the fulfillment of the promise of the definitive, fitting help that God has in store for man. The phrase "in store" suggests that one doesn't want to tell yet, one wants to keep it to oneself. This is a secret of faith that cannot yet be grasped. You cannot imagine it.

Only at the very end of His mission, at the very last moment, when He said goodbye, the day before His death, did Jesus say:

> And I will ask the Father, and he will give you another Advocate, to be with you forever. John 14:16

This Advocate is the Holy Spirit, the "Spirit of truth" (John 14:17), will "teach you everything, and remind you of all that I have said to you" (John 14:26).

It is this Spirit Who also overshadowed Mary and brought her into joyful expectation of Jesus when the Angel Gabriel announced the birth of Jesus to her. So God did not keep the Holy Spirit in store for Mary; on the contrary, she was, in biblical phrasing, the blessed one, full of grace.

When the Spirit overshadows us, too, at Pentecost, then Jesus is born in us, planted like a sunflower seed in full sunlight! In this way, God's plan comes to fruition.

In joyful expectation

So we receive much food for thought as we walk together through the increasingly bright night of our existence on the way to the Light. It gradually becomes clear that this is a spiritual Light, just as the night of our existence is a spiritual night. For example, when people are going through a difficult time of tests and ordeals, they are sometimes asked if they still see points of light.

As beings who naturally long for light, we ultimately want to see the true, the definitive and most real Light, which our whole being deeply longs for. Because this Light is our destination. We were created to meet this Light and to live in this Light and to be there in the fullest sense. This Light, which is God, is the Unity that is our triune God. We meet the Father in the Light that Jesus is as the Son, He in Whom everything was created:

The true light, which enlightens everyone, was coming into the world.

> He was in the world, and the world came into being through him; yet the world did not know him. John 1:9-10

This is the text from the beginning of the Gospel of John, which we will hear in Church on Christmas morning. Here we all find the deep, the ultimate and eternal joy, that the Book of Revelation, at the very end of the Bible, so powerfully exclaims:

> Then I saw a new heaven and a new earth; for the first heaven and the first earth had passed away, and the sea was no more. And I saw the holy city, the new Jerusalem, coming down out of heaven from God, prepared as a bride adorned for her husband. And I heard a loud voice from the throne saying, "See, the home of God is among mortals. He will dwell with them; they will be his peoples, and God himself will be with them; he will wipe every tear from their eyes. Death will be no more; mourning and crying and pain will be no more, for the first things have passed away." And the one who was seated on the throne said, "See, I am making all things new." Revelation: 21:1-5a

May we, like Mary, the Mother of the Lord, be in joyful expectation and may we hear and believe what the shepherds, sent to Bethlehem by the angels, were told:

To you is born this day in the city of David a Savior, who is the Messiah, the Lord . Luke 2:11

One of the ancient Fathers of the Church puts it this way:

> 4. For this is the night that joined, the Watchers on high with the vigil-keepers.
> The Watcher came to make watchers in the midst of creation.
> Lo! The vigil-keepers are made comrades with the Watchers: the singers of praise are made, companions of the Seraphs. Blessed be he who becomes, the harp of Your praise! and Your grace becomes his reward.
> 5. The Birth then of the Firstborn, I will sing and tell how the Godhead in the womb wove itself a vesture.
> He put it on and came forth in birth, in death again put it off — once he put it off, twice He put it on.
> On the left He wore it, then took it off thence and laid it at the right.[1]

---

[1] Ephrem the Syrian (+ 373 in Edessa). From the hymns on the Nativity. Translated by J.B. Morris (Hymn nos. 1-13) and A. Edward Johnston (Hymn nos. 14-19). From Nicene and Post-Nicene Fathers, Second Series, Vol. 13. Edited by Philip Schaff and Henry Wace. (Buffalo, NY: Christian Literature Publishing Co., 1898.) Revised and edited for New Advent by Kevin Knight. <http://www.newadvent.org/fathers/3703.htm>

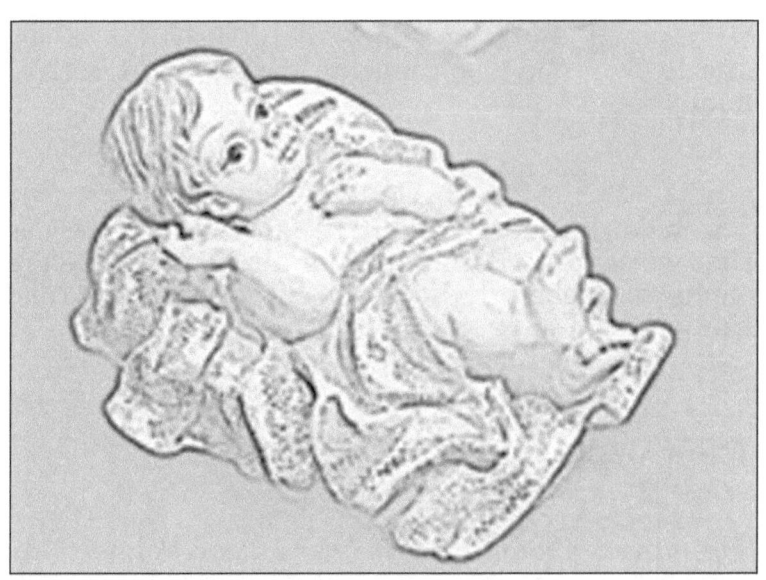

The Christmas Story: An Invitation to Us All

No matter what may have happened in the world at the end of the year, the stable in Bethlehem is as busy as ever every year. So to speak, of course.

Everyone comes to visit the newborn child, but there is something remarkable. In old paintings, there is never a burning lamp or campfire or anything like that. And yet there is light. The religious painters wanted to show that the newborn Himself is the Light. He who will later say of Himself:

> I am the Light of the world. John 8:12

He says, at the same time, to His disciples, to us, and to everyone who comes to the stable in Bethlehem:

> You are the light of the world. Matt 5:14

The beautiful thing about the Christmas story is that we see this Light, shining already, ever before we have reached the stable in Bethlehem. You read that right. We are going to Bethlehem.

The Gospel and our Life story

The stories about Jesus in the Gospels relate to today, and even more, tomorrow. So the older we get, the more vital and current this old story becomes.

Similarly, our own life story is not dead but living and dynamic—it's not yet finished, and I don't mean in terms of our life span, the number of our days. Our life story is not yet finished because we still do not fully know ourselves. There's something kept in store for us: the secret of who we are.

However beautiful our life may be, a veil still hides that deeper knowledge of who we are, really, in the true sense. There's still a kind of darkness around us, a kind of nighttime. In the middle of the night, an old and wise Jewish scholar, Nicodemus, comes to Jesus. Jesus says to him:

> Very truly, I tell you, no one can see the kingdom of God without being born from above. John 3:3

Nicodemus then asks:

> How can anyone be born after having grown old? Can one enter a second time into the mother's womb and be born? John 3:4

He speaks, indeed, on behalf of all of us. The Christmas story gives the answer to this question. While telling about the birth of Jesus, Christmas becomes our personal story, as well. So, the gospel is meant as the good news for each of us, for me.

The Christmas story is also about our birth. About our being born again, and coming to life, in our current circumstances, no matter how young or old we are. To be born again relates to our actual life, right now, as well as to our death and what follows afterward.

The night brings clear insight

At night, in the darkness, where the divine Light is not yet visible, Jesus tells old Nicodemus that he will catch the (in)sight of the depth of his life through his rebirth.

As for our own birth: we all have come into the world, but we no longer remember anything about it. At birth, we step out of the darkness of the womb towards the light. This happens with every birth. A child is born with closed eyes and closed lungs. As soon as the lungs breathe air, life enters that little human being, who opens her or his eyes for the first time.

Jesus speaks of a rebirth in a completely different way. Then we will be fully conscious and we will know what's in store for us.
Even though you have reached a ripe old age, just like old Nicodemus, a rebirth still awaits you. What

does this mean? Jesus speaks about life now and John the Baptist about the future.

Jesus says about the current life:

> But those who do what is true come to the light, so that it may be clearly seen that their deeds have been done in God. John 3:21

And about the near future, John the Baptist says:

> Whoever believes in the Son has eternal life. John 3:36

Christmas as an image of our life

Sincere faith awakens the human being, while well-meaning good deeds call us to new life. Indeed, a person becomes human according to God's original intention and idea. From this perspective, the Christmas story can be read anew: as a striking image, a metaphor of one's own origins and future.

Dreams in the night

And again it becomes night. Joseph dreams of an angel, who reassures him about accepting Mary as his wife. In this way, the angel gives him a rebirth, so that the prediction by the Prophet Isaiah of so long ago comes true for Joseph:

> Look, the young woman [virgin] is with child and shall bear a son, and shall name him Immanuel. Isaiah 7:14

This dream was so clear and powerful that Joseph no longer doubted. He converted this certainty into action, action done in God, by standing up as the bridegroom of the Blessed Virgin Mary. What's beautiful about the story is how Joseph is very much like us. Like Joseph, we also struggle with doubts of all kinds regarding our faith.

The Wise Men in that same night

Wise men from the East, scientists and astronomers, see a bright star, which points to the new King of the Jews—of that they are certain. Would they really have made such a long desert journey if this newborn King had no royal significance for them, too?

We are in their good company as seekers of Him whom we have not yet seen. After a long search and questioning, the wise men finally succeed in finding the King's child in Bethlehem and they offer Him their gifts. Their presumption has proved true.

Angels appear

And at the same time, shepherds in the nearby area also experienced a wonderful night. Not a dream, but an appearance of a legion of angels, as numerous as the stars in the sky, carrying an unmistakable and irrefutable message:

> To you is born this day in the city of David a Savior, who is the Messiah, the Lord. Luke 2:11

Today, today! The Bible always talks about the current day, here and now, given as long as you live on earth. Even the simple shepherds, people like all of us, were born again in their own way:

> The shepherds returned, glorifying and praising God for all they had heard and seen, as it had been told them. Luke 2:20

The Human Being sleeps, but the Creator does not

Once again, night falls, and once again, there are plenty of dreams: the wise men from the East dream that they must avoid and ignore the jealous King Herod. That same night, Joseph also has a new dream. He is strongly advised to flee to Egypt together with Mary, his wife, and the child Jesus.

Again and again, during the nighttime, God seems best able to reach humankind. This was evident with the first human in the creation story, as mentioned above:

> So the Lord God caused a deep sleep to fall upon the man, and he slept; then he took one of his ribs and closed up its place with flesh. And the rib that the Lord God had taken from the man he made into a woman and brought her to the man. Genesis 2:21-22

When humankind rests, the Creator becomes active. The night apparently lends itself to rebirth. So for Nicodemus, the wise men from the East, and the shepherds. It is also during the night, the Night of Nights, the Easter Night, when Jesus will rise again. The Bible reminds us, again and again, in this way, that God created both the day and the night. So, even in the night of war and misery, God is present!

Angels

The Bible describes angels as invisible guardians; they stand before God's throne. They are messengers from another world. Angels sometimes appear in dreams, or when mortal danger threatens. They wish to tell or give a message, lift and carry us, when we are in pain and sorrow.

In youth, people were familiar with the belief in a guardian angel. In itself that's a very beautiful notion, especially in our unsafe world. Everyone has their own security guard, their own bodyguard: Imagine that!

The Bible refers to the idea in three places.

The Book of Exodus says:

> I am going to send an angel in front of you, to guard you on the way and to bring you to the place that I have prepared. Exodus 23:20

In the Book of Psalms, we read:

> The angel of the Lord encamps around those who fear him, and delivers them. Psalm 34:7

And Jesus says, according to the Gospel of Matthew:

> Take care that you do not despise one of these little ones; for, I tell you, in heaven their angels continually see the face of my Father in heaven. Matt 18:10

These three texts may have given rise to the belief in guardian angels. On Russian icons, they are often depicted, on the edges surrounding the central icon, together with the names of saints recalling family members. In this way, angels and saints are given the status of family members, symbolically, you could say. Good company never goes away! Literally.

Good company, however, stands or falls with frequent contact. Decades ago, many believers still had a personal missal, from which they prayed daily. They were treasure chests full of spiritual riches. Prayer cards of deceased family members, for example, were kept in them. Such prayer books often contained the following Prayer to the Guardian Angel:

O faithful guide, whom God has given me
As my protector and keeper.
What gratitude do I not owe you
For all the care, faithfulness and love

That you daily show me?
When I sleep, you watch over me.
When I am sad, you comfort me.
When I become fainthearted, you strengthen me.
In danger, you help me.
In doubt, you counsel me.
You keep me from evil and lead me to good.
You stir me up to repentance
And reconcile me with God.

I pray you, never leave me,
Comfort me in adversity, protect me in danger,
Come to my aid in temptations,
So that I may never be overwhelmed by them.
Bring all my prayers and good works
Before the Divine Face,
And make me inherit/possess eternal life
After this transitory life ends.

Amen

Mrs. Den Hartogh

Speaking of angels, my parental home was in the See Hero District in The Hague. It is a stately mansion, with large rooms, decorative frills on the ceilings, without a garden, yet with a back balcony.

Over the railing from the left balcony, the Peace Palace was visible, and to the right, in the distance, the tower of the big church called St. James. But closer still, and most meaningful, on summer days, was the sight of Mrs. Den Hartogh, standing in her flower garden. This was a small city garden, yet with the stature of the Botanical Garden of Lisse.

The most beautiful flower in this garden was Mrs. Den Hartogh herself, who lived happily there with her husband in their small ground-floor apartment. She always waved enthusiastically when we called to her as children. Then, we'd stop by to receive a nice treat. My two sisters and I would do that immediately, of course.

To enter was to be in a party atmosphere. The flowers were not only in her garden but everywhere in the house: on the wallpaper, curtains, and carpeting. Even her dresses had a floral pattern. The small living room was cozy, neat, and tidy.

Mr. Den Hartogh sat in a large armchair by the stove. When we came in, he would say: "Oh, I can already hear who is there. You look beautiful!"

When we got a bit older, I dared to ask him: "Why do you always have that white stick with the red stripes with you?"
He said, "Oh, I will tell you. I have two helpers. One is my dear wife and the other is this dear stick, because when you are blind you need an extra sense."

"But how is that possible?" I asked him, "You always say that we look so beautiful."
"Well," he said, "That is the secret of blind people. They see by listening."
I didn't understand it at all, but I remembered.

On our birthday, Mrs. Den Hartogh put a beautifully decorated card, inscribed with Bible verses, in the mailbox. I kept her cards for a long time, but I don't know now where I may have them.

When I was a student, Mr. Den Hartogh passed away. Mrs. Den Hartog could no longer live on her own and had to go to the nursing home. I went to visit her there once during my Christmas vacation. The flowers were everywhere, in the interior and on her dress, but no longer in her eyes. She had now become a little blind like her husband. She said she could no longer see him. I sympathized with her grief. Shortly afterwards, she also passed away, happily, because she went to be with her husband, she said, since he had recently passed away.

And now that I have grown older myself, I'm aware that in my youth I had already been visiting Paradise, around the corner on Hugo de Groot street, where those two angels lived. It's too bad they never had children of their own.

Walking and wondering

Poets and writers, painters and artists, have been inspired by nature throughout the centuries. The light, the colors, and the beauty of nature are tremendous.

During a walk, people encounter things that resemble what's familiar to them or remind them of their life story. Anyone who takes a walk is, as it were, walking through their own diary. All kinds of memories come to the surface, as things both small and big catch your notice along the way. Anyone who is receptive to the transcendent and its messages will absorb that as a kind of nourishment and supplement to their inner self. A walk is therefore recommended not only to keep us fit but it for refreshment.

Whether you walk alone, enjoying the silence, or walk with another or in a group, enjoying and getting to know one another, nature and the walkers are linked in a tender embrace.
During the corona virus period, it was suddenly no longer possible to fly to distant countries, to spend a great deal of money. Many compatriots have rediscovered our own homeland. Years ago, they considered it absolutely impossible to 'just stay in the Netherlands'. When they had no other choice, many started walking. Days have passed, sometimes weeks in a row, and many have been asking themselves: "Why didn't we do this before?"

Walking brings people back to the simplicity of life. You can't take more with you than you can carry in your backpack. You don't plan a night's accommodation in a place that is miles away from your route. Along the way, you learn to live with what is there and that is actually enough. All luxury seems to be a thing of the past. Because what could be better than getting up with the sun and going to bed at sunset? The walker, participating in nature directly, cultivates an ear and an eye to sense what he would otherwise rush past. And so, people automatically come to themselves, to who they really are.

Conserving and Preserving

Conserving (i.e. self-preservation) keeps us busy in a latent way. We usually don't worry consciously so much; yet, subconsciously, we worry: "Where will my beautiful things that I have cherished with so much love, be? Where shall they move to?" These are belongings that carry personal recollections. However, we conserve not only our things.

Conserving and preserving in all shapes and sizes

We have all kinds of words for conserving, such as: saving, reserving, preserving, storing, maintaining, guarding, covering, protecting, safeguarding, sheltering. To show how we prioritize conserving or self-preservation, consider our interest in preferably maintaining good health and, yes, conserving or preserving it.

As a child

As a child you could be completely absorbed in very simple and basic hobbies that had to do with conserving and preserving, such as collecting stamps, coins, cigar bands, and pins, as if your life depended on it. You collected mainly to exchange and thus collect even more.

Vital conservation and preservation

The above activities are just pastimes to find a bit of peace. Of course, there are also vital forms of preservation and conservation. For example, we casually open the refrigerator to take out food that would not reach the end of its designated shelf life without refrigeration. And that refrigerator only fills up when we empty our wallets, where we keep our money, at the supermarket checkout.
Are there forms of conservation and preservation that are even more important?, you might wonder.

Yes, there are, certainly! What about your photo albums with all those precious snapshots from the past? My mother always said (after the Christmas tree had caught fire): "If there ever should be a fire, we must at least make sure that the photo albums are saved." After all, thanks to photos, all kinds of sweet memories come to the surface, especially when loved ones are no longer around.

Cherishing memories

When it comes to preserving memories, cherishing comes first, indicating a deeper dimension. To remember is to take into yourself, again and again, that which is in danger of being forgotten. Is that why you have beautifully framed photos hanging in your room? Friendly faces of the many present in your life, or those who have passed away, sadly, but whose memory is kept in your heart?

The heart is a repository of more than just good memories, however. Unintentionally, the heart is a repository also of everything that you want to forget—whatever you would rather not talk about, because it is too difficult or because of shame.

Sharing memories and thoughts means giving them to another for safekeeping. This will be someone you trust completely. Otherwise, if your trust is betrayed, you will be hurt even more.

The other side of the story

To be honest, not all memories should be kept if they are disruptive and stand in the way of joy. People may cling, almost possessively, to an unpleasant word that they once heard. For example, a pastor once made a remark perceived as insulting, and, from that time, all of the faith and Church were cast in a negative light. We may tend to prove ourselves right by attention to those who do not really engage with us in conversation, but who only talk at us. Some people, it seems, do not want to get rid of their unpleasant memories. They keep walking around carrying a backpack full of unpleasantness—an unwise kind of keeping, which invites a question regarding the nature of wisdom.

Keeping value, valuable

Clearly, keeping has a link with truth, what is real, what really exists, what's fundamental to your life. And what about the person himself?

We come to a core question, which determines our entire self-understanding:
Are human beings, you and I, worthy of being kept and preserved?

This question has occupied minds for centuries, though it's also surrounded by many doubts:
"Do you really believe that heaven exists?" someone asked me recently. She had lost her husband and two sons. "What do you think?" she asked, "Will I ever see them again, high up in heaven?" Her question contained the answer. The lady had not ruled out this possibility.

Maintaining relationships

The Bible speaks, in various tones, about God's intention to protect and preserve the human being in the ultimate sense. The theme of conserving or preserving appears to be important in the Bible, beginning with Paradise.

> The Lord God took the man and put him in the garden of Eden to till it and keep it. Genesis 2:15

In the ancient language of the Bible, Hebrew, this verse contains the verb shamar (pronounced shamar) which pertains to observing and maintaining; so it's a kind of vigilant preservation of God's goodness and commandments, with the goal of returning them to the owner in the same or even better condition. Ultimately, the benefits are for the human soul. So that humans may stay on track, we are reminded to be just as occupied with God's Word as with our own good health.

The faithful person preserves God's Word by translating the Word into actions. God as our Preserver gives us His Word to keep so that the human being is ultimately kept (i.e., preserved) in all thought, action and omission.

A word with multiple meanings

Sometimes in biblical translations, instead of 'keep' or 'preserve', translations are given such as 'guard' in the sense of the Latin observatio, which means to observe or to keep a close eye on.

The translation with the terms 'preserve' or 'keep' seem appropriate, because what's precious and dear is meant to be preserved, and people wish to do it, just as the Monuments Watch inspects all monumental buildings, from time to time, so that they are conserved and preserved, because "we want to preserve these buildings for posterity."

God protects life

After the fall, the human being is sent away from Paradise and an angel stands at the gate, to "guard the way to the tree of life" (Genesis 3:24). This was to prevent the human from picking from that tree, too. The result would have been that evil in its human form would continue to exist forever, and therefore be preserved. That is exactly what God does not want. Although human beings had to be expelled from Paradise, the story says, God continued to watch over us, with tenderness, and to keep us. The naked person is personally clothed by God (verse 21), just as your mother used to do when you went to school: "Put on your coat and your scarf, because it is cold outside and otherwise you will get sick."

Preserving in the Bible in a broader sense

In the Bible, much is preserved in the law. There are cases where someone has given an ox or a donkey to another for safekeeping. Or the herd is pastured and preserved, that is, guarded. And the people? They are kept or preserved for a certain task or destination in their service to God. In short, preserving is really a most important theme in the Bible. You could almost say: everything stands or falls with this!

Preserving your soul

Ultimately, we go from the small to the great. We as humans receives the Promised Land on condition that we will "keep God's commandments". And they are there not to be forgotten! So imprint them on your heart or print them on paper. They are stated clearly and powerfully, here is a text to hang framed above your bed:

> But take care and watch yourselves closely, so as neither to forget the things that your eyes have seen nor to let them slip from your mind all the days of your life; make them known to your children and your children's children. Deuteronomy 4:9

This seems to be a core fact for man: you can wish to keep all sorts of things in your life, but what matters is to keep both the divine guidelines and your own soul and that is even more important than maintaining good health.
You could say that life is about keeping an eye on what matters to both God and people from their deepest core. Jesus says it in His own way:

> For what will it profit them to gain the whole world and forfeit their life? Indeed, what can they give in return for their life?
> Mark 8:36-37

To keep your soul is only possible within the greater whole or entirety of God's all-encompassing love. And just as parents must remain involved with their children, so God remains closely involved with people, too. God wants to keep man, and that is why the praying person cries out to God:

> Guard me as the apple of the eye;
> hide me in the shadow of your wings.
> Psalm 17:8

Finally

In the Bible, in principle human beings will never disappear forever into some great black hole of absolute nothingness. The human being is called to be as good as God. That is a condition of existence.

So it is *quid pro quo.* The Bible is about keeping, preserving, and saving, for now and for later; it's about protecting and conserving until the end of the ages, the age to come. Then, the ages will no longer be experienced as an eternity, because time, evil, and death will no longer exist. Thank God! The text of Psalm 121 is a striking example. Actually, this is a beautiful text to pray daily. You are given time, hours, and days, while you look forward to the blessed fulfillment of your hope!

Psalm 121

~ States Translation ~

I lift up my eyes to the hills—
  from where will my help come?
2 My help comes from the Lord,
  who made heaven and earth.
3 He will not let your foot be moved;
  he who keeps you will not slumber.
4 He who keeps Israel
  will neither slumber nor sleep.
5 The Lord is your keeper;
  the Lord is your shade at your right hand.
6 The sun shall not strike you by day,
  nor the moon by night.
7 The Lord will keep you from all evil;
  he will keep your life.
8 The Lord will keep
  your going out and your coming in
  from this time on and forevermore.

Experiencing loss

No one grows old without suffering loss. The experience of loss is simply a part of our temporary existence. The loss of loved ones is usually the most profound. People have shared joys and sorrows for years. They are linked, having become each other in heart and soul—you could say. They may begin to resemble each other, speak each other's words, read each other's thoughts and know each other's habits. And suddenly all of that ends, and you are left alone, with your heart full of memories. That is a great shock, to put it mildly.

It is worth mentioning those, in particular, who have already lost one or more of their own children.

The only slight consolation, at that time, is to recall that the lasting feeling of loss is an unmistakable sign of love, a living love beyond death. The feeling of loss does not have to wear off, no matter what people say, when it is impatiently suggested, "Isn't it time that....?"

To miss someone is essentially to long for a reunion, for being together again as it once was: the look in the eyes, the sound of voice, the way they enter the room, the touch, that loving kiss. To experience your loss intensely is very good.

Ask yourself this question: "Why is my feeling of loss so strong?" The question is not meant to keep you brooding but for you to consider in peace. This can last for a while; give yourself the space for reflection. Reflection is necessary so that one may come to rest. It is like a good night's sleep, which one has not had for a while. After such reflection, one can naturally focus the attention again on daily life. In this way, life revives like a new spring. And the loss? That is not gone, fortunately, but has now taken up residence, in a good place. within the heart.

If your sense of loss diminishes, do not blame yourself. Believe that your loved one is being kept by the Father in heaven until you meet again, on the day when the sun will no longer go down.
The more precious someone is in your life, the greater the loss. "Life goes on!" is shouted sooner or later. Yes, but the question is how then? In what way?

On the one hand, there are people who never get over a great loss. On the other hand, people can be extremely down-to-earth, and they will literally say, they've anticipated a certain loss all their life. It should be clear that one person is not the same as another. There must be mutual respect. Be that as it may, in the art of life, one learns to deal with loss

in style. This seems easy to say, of course, but the daily reality is often very different. Serious losses usually take years to get over—just somewhat.
Loss is a process with its own dynamics, which you cannot accelerate by will. There is a natural growth process with a built-in rhythm. Similarly, a physical wound takes time to heal. The more one is aware of the healing process, spiritually, and learns to live with it, the more smoothly it will proceed.

To process loss occurs in phases that sometimes overlap:

1. Denial

Initially there is a phase of denial:
- "It can't be true!"
- "I never thought this would happen to me!"
- "I didn't see it coming!"

Eventually, the new reality cannot be denied and the next phase begins.

2. Anger and rage

Anger comes from feeling wronged. This anger is usually directed at the people closest to you in the immediate environment:
- "My daughter just made me move out of my flat and now I'm sitting here in this little room."
- "They think I can't do anything anymore, but I've always been very independent/very much on my own."
- "I love my boyfriend, but behind my back he goes to that other woman."

In this phase, people sometimes suppose that it is wrong to be angry or furious. But as long as there's no violence, to express anger can be very justified and even have a healing effect. Anger is therefore, clearly, a useful emotion. You distance yourself, as it were, from the disappointment you've had to endure. Expressing anger and rage nonviolently has a beneficial impact. You communicate, honestly, to another, and to yourself, the cause of your great pain. It is right to speak about this, in a good way, and to express yourself.

Reflecting on our anger may bring us to question the origins of that anger, and our feelings of loss. This is a personal reflection and a thinking for ourselves. It is wise not to suppress anger, lest the anger should suddenly explode at an unguarded moment, uncontrolled with undesirable consequences. Anyone dealing with losses and grieving, at the same time, should hopefully find a confidante, with whom to talk in good faith. For example, within the short period of just a few months, one can lose their partner, home, and good health, while the loss of a pet can also be very drastic. There will then occur three or four grieving processes, simultaneously, while family and acquaintances will usually only acknowledge the loss of the partner! It should be remembered that people deal with the grieving process in their own way. Each person is an individual unlike another. After the stage of anger and rage, a period of doubt and hesitation follows.

3. Doubting and hesitating

After the worst anger, there arises the question: "What will another person say about this?" During an encouraging conversation, it will hopefully become clear that to mourn a loss does not mean a loss of face. The phase of doubting is the time for gnawing uncertainty and confusion. The storm of anger and rage may have subsided, but true inner peace still seems far away. That is not surprising, for the most important phase is yet to come, namely the actual grief itself.

4. Grief

Beyond doubts and hesitation, there is room for a deeper pain and tears: What about your grief exactly? What do I miss the most? What was actually most dear to me? Anger, denial, and brooding often amount to suppressed pains that we bottle up. But this phase of grief can last quite a long time. Not everyone grieves for the same amount of time. This can vary from person to person from days and weeks, to months, or even years. The processing of a loss is complex and complicated. You want to go on with your life, but it just doesn't seem to work.

Eventually, a feeling of resignation will come. Whether you want it or not, you just accept the given situation. So there's still no real resolution or freedom to feel happy again. This will come in the next phase, that of acceptance.

5. Acknowledgement and acceptance

Doubts, sadness, and anger have all been experienced. The worst seems to be over, at least somewhat. A certain peace has arrived. You know that reality is not nice, but you can go along with it. You give it a place and you think of the beautiful moments in and out of life. Maybe you will manage to pick up the thread of life, again, at least a little.

Meaning after loss

"Dad, you should not grieve for what is over, but be grateful for what you have experienced!," my son, who was 14 at that time, once said to me. When asked from whom he got that wisdom, he replied that he had come up with it himself. This wisdom helped me to look at loss differently. A different perspective allows you to see life in a different light. A serious loss does not necessarily have only negative aspects in the long run.

A while ago, in the mornings, I used to visit a widow who had lost her husband as a result of an accident, just a couple of years after their wedding day. At the time, she had to raise their young children by herself, from one day to the next. The loss of her husband had made her family and her bond with other families very close and intense.

In the afternoons, I used to visit another widow. She had moved to her new care facility, just two years previously, after the death of her husband. They had been married for no less than 62 years and they were able to celebrate their 60th wedding anniversary with many people. This last widow experienced her double grief very strongly: no more husband after all those years and no more home, on top of that, given her recent move to a care facility. It was all a bit too much at once. Of course, I had to think of the life story of the widow I had visited that morning. Everyone has his or her own sorrow and loss and feels it in different ways.

To support and give attention to acquaintances, friends, or housemates is of great importance. You can mean so much to each other. No one has been spared suffering and loss. Hopefully, this shared experience will create a strong bond anew with fellow human beings.

It's incredibly important to work together to create a pleasant atmosphere in your home or in your family. Every resident—without exception!—comes in with a dose of loss. You can help each other bear that burden.

Ascending to the Light

About Candlemas, the Feast of the Presentation of the Lord in the Temple

The ancient feast of Candlemas, traditionally celebrated on 2 February, marks the 40th day after the birth of Jesus. And to put more emphasis on the Lord himself and not just on His mother Mary, this feast is now called the Feast of the Presentation of the Lord in the Temple. A unique component of the celebration of this feast in church is that of the faithful wait, in the portal for the Mass, with a candle in their hands. Together with Mary and Joseph and the little Jesus, who is the light of the world, they enter the temple.

The Gospel story of this day

At the end of Advent and the Christmas season, this biblical narrative captures the atmosphere of the holidays and it is meant to be heard again and again:

> 22 When the time came for their purification according to the law of Moses, they brought him up to Jerusalem to present him to the Lord
> 23 (as it is written in the law of the Lord, "Every firstborn male shall be designated as holy to the Lord"),
> 24 and they offered a sacrifice according to what is stated in the law of the Lord, "a pair of turtledoves or two young pigeons."
> 25 Now there was a man in Jerusalem whose name was Simeon; this man was righteous and devout, looking forward to the consolation of Israel, and the Holy Spirit rested on him.
> 26 It had been revealed to him by the Holy Spirit that he would not see death before he had seen the Lord's Messiah.
> 27 Guided by the Spirit, Simeon came into the temple; and when the parents brought in the child Jesus, to do for him what was customary under the law,
> 28 Simeon took him in his arms and praised God, saying,
> 29 "Master, now you are dismissing your servant in peace,
>   according to your word;
> 30 for my eyes have seen your salvation,
> 31 which you have prepared in the presence of all peoples,
> 32 a light for revelation to the Gentiles
>   and for glory to your people Israel."

33 And the child's father and mother were amazed at what was being said about him. 34 Then Simeon blessed them and said to his mother Mary, "This child is destined for the falling and the rising of many in Israel, and to be a sign that will be opposed 35 so that the inner thoughts of many will be revealed—and a sword will pierce your own soul too."
36 There was also a prophet, Anna the daughter of Phanuel, of the tribe of Asher. She was of a great age, having lived with her husband seven years after her marriage, 37 then as a widow to the age of eighty-four. She never left the temple but worshiped there with fasting and prayer night and day. 38 At that moment she came, and began to praise God and to speak about the child to all who were looking for the redemption of Jerusalem.
39 When they had finished everything required by the law of the Lord, they returned to Galilee, to their own town of Nazareth.
40 The child grew and became strong, filled with wisdom; and the favor of God was upon him. Luke 2:22-40

In this story, people of all ages, from young to old, play an important role. This story connects all generations and invites us to search for what life is all about.

Candlemas

Initially, the church celebration of this feast was simply called Candlemas, inspired by what old Simeon saw: 'the Light that shines for the Gentiles.' We as non-Jewish people are those Gentiles, but what is that Light for us? For the Jews themselves, it was like a 'glory to your people Israel'.

Light and glory. "Long will you live in glory" (gloria) is sung on your birthday. This glory, gloria, means glory, God's Glory. Simeon presents the child Jesus before God's face:

Simeon took him in his arms and praised God, saying,

> Master, now you are dismissing your servant in peace,
>   according to your word;
> for my eyes have seen your salvation,
>   which you have prepared in the presence of all peoples,
>   a light for revelation to the Gentiles
>   and for glory to your people Israel.
> Luke 2:28-32

To paraphrase, Simeon's blessing means: "May this human child also be Your child." It is a confirmation and recognition that children are indeed gifts from God.

Old Simeon and Anna remind us that the essence of life may become visible as a Light only in the very last phase of our lives, after having experienced so much of life.

This sounds very nice, certainly, but the daily reality is usually very different. The older you get, the more aimless life can feel. This is partly because so many of your loved ones have already died before you.

Aimlessness of life

"I am already so old, even my children have died and my grandchildren live far away and are all busy," someone said to me recently. There was nothing left to live for or look forward to. "My life is becoming boring," someone else said.

"Just pray for a blessed death for me," my father said, every time we said goodbye. His prayer was indeed answered! Perhaps it is a good idea to dust off that old concept of blessed death and explore it in more depth. The Feast of the Presentation of the Lord in the temple provides vital inspiration for a joyful perspective on the end of life.

The Blessed Death

Every person with a death wish has, at the core, a life wish, namely a desire for a good life. The desire for death emerges from the daily realization that this earthly life is transient, in all respects, finite, and without prospects. This process of life is irreversible, and that realization cannot be refuted. On the contrary, hopefully it will be taken seriously by all loved ones.

The wish for a speedy death is justified and self-evident. To be allowed to die, without lengthy suffering, is then that blessed death. Blessedness is a specific Christian idea of redemption, from this overly limited, earthly life. A blessed life is life beyond earthly existence.

The blessed death is actually what old Simeon might have longed for, but not until he had glimpsed with his own eyes God's Salvation in the person of the long-awaited Messiah:

> Master, now you are dismissing your servant in peace,
> according to your word; for my eyes have seen your salvation,
> which you have prepared in the presence of all peoples. Luke 2:29-31

That passionate prayer was finally answered. The holy Simeon must have died his blessed death. With Simeon's words of gratitude, monks in their monasteries close their day every day.

For us, the words may close not only the day, but above all, a life.

The farewell to the Nativity scene

The second of February, as mentioned, concludes the forty-day Christmas season. It is time to pack up the last remaining Nativity scenes and entrust them to the attic in peace.

In his last days, Simeon was allowed to look the little newborn Messiah in the eyes. Hence, the Eastern Churches prefer to call this feast, very concisely: Encounter of the Lord. Simeon held a great Mystery in his hands. He was appointed to dedicate the little Jesus to God on behalf of all humanity. What emotion must have arisen in this man of God!

He saw a great Light in Jesus, but, at that time, he probably didn't even know that he carried more in his hands than just the Messiah of Israel. Jesus would manifest and reveal himself as the Son of God, as Savior or Redeemer. These last two titles risk disappearing completely from our language of faith as well as the meaningful world evoked by it.

Our world seems to be turning inward by a persistent self-satisfaction. For many, the content of the Christian faith no longer matters deeply, namely for truly liberating and redeeming the human from evil, sin, and, by extension, death—a liberation given so that one may partake of the divine life.

Christian faith seems be an antique idea in the meantime—like the images of the Nativity, which disappear into the attic and are finally given away by relatives to the thrift shop.

Remarkably, despite this, we are convinced of the power of evil and all the world's. We will never deny their existence. And even people who no longer believe say, "Why doesn't God do anything about the misery in the world, if He exists?"

The newborn meets God

And that is exactly what God does. He does everything He can to free us humans from all the negativity and all the Evil (with a capital E). God wants to offer us perspective. People who in their utmost desperation beg God for help receive it. That is why Jesus is called the Redeemer, the Healer, or the Savior. The entire mission of Jesus, and message, revolve around homecoming; precisely, we human beings are brought home by God. To come home assuredly means to meet God.

What was taught in the past

Many older people wonder how concepts such as primordial sin, purgatory, and indulgences relate to the end of life. These are concepts the Church spoke about often in their youth.
They are thought about variously in Christianity. The Eastern Churches, for example, have no official church doctrine at all relating to these three concepts. They say that a blessed death refers both to our death in the flesh and to our life in God in general.

The human being is called to live in God from birth. Death is then like the transition from Good Friday to Easter.

Arriving at your destination

The long journey of your life is approaching its destination. As soon as the final station comes into view, you hear the conductor call out: "You are all requested to get off or change. And don't forget to take your luggage with you."

By the way, as far as luggage and dying are concerned, one centenarian said that in Friesland, they used to have the following proverb for those who were overly attached to earthly goods: "The last shirt has no pockets indeed." That referred to the shroud with which the deceased were dressed, which had no pockets, because what would you put into them?

This is your blessed death. You arrive at your destination, and there, He Who is your life is waiting.

He is there to receive you, He Who loves you to the depths of His Heart, He Who looks out for you and welcomes you home.

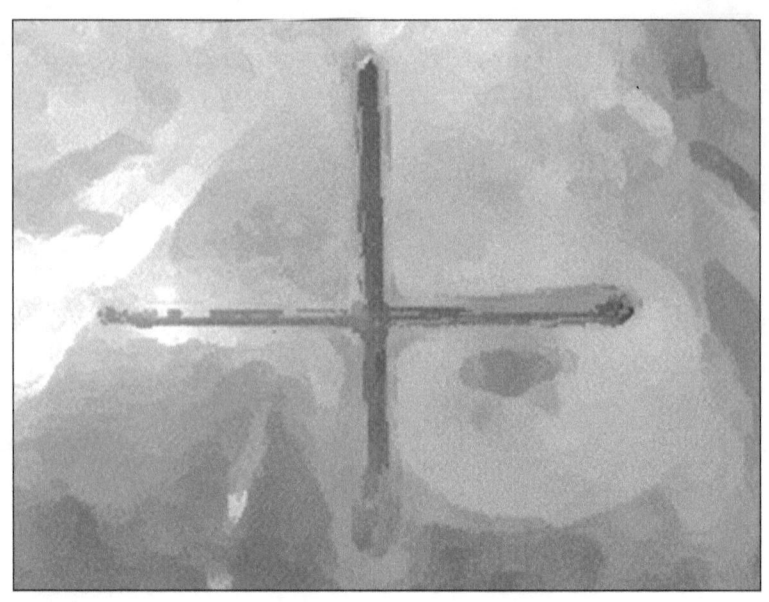

Prayer for a blessed death

Finally, on the next page, a prayer to Him, Who is your destination as a believer.
A prayer for a blessed death is good and more than justified.

Prayer for a blessed death

Father in heaven,
Jesus told us
'Whatever you ask the Father in My name,
He will give you.'
Therefore I ask You:
Please bring me home to You in Your house
with the many dwellings,
of which Jesus said

that He will prepare a place for us there,
Where there will be no more weeping and no more pain,
because all that is old will be finished there.

I have tried to live well and to be a good person for my fellow human beings, but please forgive me where I was not focused on them, but only on myself, in my moments of darkness.

I want to trust in Your merciful Love. Please send me Your angels, and all my loved ones, who have gone before me, grant that they may all accompany me on the path to You, on the path to Your loving Father's heart.

Please take me into Your Kingdom, O Lord,
And let me arrive into Your divine Light,
which dispels all darkness.

All the fruits of the talents that You have given me,
I want to offer to You, as the evening sacrifice of my life. Please accept them, O Lord, as my contribution to the coming of Your Kingdom, to Your praise and to the honor of Jesus' Holy Name.

Bless everyone I have met, especially my dearest ones. Keep them in Your goodness and stay close to them in this farewell.

Holy Triune God,
Let me be born again in the eternal Light,
that I may see You as You are.

Amen

Pain

Pain for many people is a daily reality that they are forced to live with; for many of you, day and night, it is very difficult to imagine living without pain. Moreover, discomfort comes in the form of itching, dizziness, nausea, moodiness, depression, and side effects of your medication.

Pain is much more than just a bad feeling. That is why it is so difficult to talk about pain. And others are quick to give you so-called good advice that doesn't interest and does very little for you.

Do you want to talk about pain or not, and with whom? The dilemma lies there. It is not advisable to suppress what you feel. Pain can lead to feelings of loneliness because "my pain, which I have, someone else does not have, or at least has it differently."

At the same time, pain can also give a feeling of a common and shared experience. Talking about our pain in a constructive way is like the age-old sharing of joys and sorrows, as you do in a relationship with fellow human beings.

Heartache

Pain seems invisible, but usually it is not. A single word, a certain look in the eyes, or the sound of someone's voice can indicate how someone is feeling.

In addition to physical pain, there is mental pain. Sadness, for example, can express itself in different ways depending on its depth. Grief that has arisen years ago can remain deeply embedded in the emotional life.

One grief is not the same as another. What is the grief of a woman, married for 67 years, having suddenly lost her husband, home, and freedom within a short timespan? It is a very different grief from that of someone whose children have broken off contact in anger. The pain is equal, of course, no less in either case. Every person's pain is individual and their grief unique. The pain of missing a close partner was beautifully and aptly expressed by Toon Hermans:

The last look:

I witnessed a sober funeral. A large, strong man of around sixty stood at his wife's grave. When the coffin had sunk into the ground and the handful of family members turned away from the grave, the man stood there for a moment. I was standing about four meters away from him. He cast a last look at the grave and I heard him mumble with a tear in his voice: "Goodbye oldy." Never before have I heard love expressed so clearly in two words.[2]

Forgotten

There is also a form of very sharp pain when two people have known each other for so long and suddenly one of them starts to show unusual behaviors. The writer J. Bernlef tells of this, very softly and lovingly, in his novel *Chimeras*[3], in which Maarten, the man, seems to become increasingly forgetful:

Robert stands up and stretches with his front legs outstretched next to the central heating and then slowly approaches me. Without knowing it, dogs have a built-in clock. They sense exactly when they need to be let out. I stroke his back briefly, against the hairs of his smooth coat.

"You're right, Robert, it's time for our daily walk."

"You've already done that, Maarten."

Vera's face is red and her lips are thin and tight under her sharp nose, the nose of an old woman suddenly, with a small white, bloodless tip.

"Really, you've forgotten, but you've already let him out."

I look at the dog hesitantly, but it seems as if Vera is right this time because Robert settles down again next to the central heating in his familiar spot. So that must be right. Animals cannot lie.

---

2 Toon Hermans, Fluiten naar de overkant (Whistling towards another side) Editor: Elsevier – Amsterdam/Brussel (1974); ISBN: 9789010030115; Paperback, 192 p. (1982), p.138. Translated by Guram Kochi MSc

3 J. Bernlef, Hersenschimmen (Chimeras), Wolters-Noordhoff, 1990

"I am forgetful, aren't I?"
"I love you just the way you are," she says. "It doesn't matter."

Then I get up, because I suddenly, very suddenly have to pee. Hot stitches in my lower body. Where do they come from so suddenly? What is lurking inside my body that it has its sights set on me?

Fear of dementia

That great and most frightening suffering for many elderly people is the threat of losing your mental faculties. That's a hard blow. The inability to remember the names of your fellow human beings is one thing, when it comes to distant figures or acquaintances, such as those on television. But when you start to forget the names of closer friends and family members, serious doubts begin to arise.

It is typical to ask: "I am forgetful, aren't I?" And it not only sounds like the expression of an inner pain, but also of a sadness, for apparently, you are no longer able to be who you think or thought you were, indeed who you are and have been. Let us hope there will be someone to say: "I love you, just the way you are." So, in other words: "For me, you are, and will remain my darling".

That is what love does in a situation like this. Fortunately, love appears to have many deeper layers. The loving person discovers a much greater reservoir of compassionate sympathy within him or herself than was previously believed possible.
Parents who have had a mentally handicapped child from birth know this all too well. In fact, you discover, all the more, how a person is a being of love. To

stand next to someone with dementia will be a very complex, usually, and intensive. And yet, not only does this person's life change, with his illness, but also those of the closest family members. It is then to be hoped, and desired, that in everything, mutual relationships will become stronger and people will grow together, with as little alienation as possible, even where feelings sometimes tend in that direction. To be human is greater and more profound than the current circumstances that seem to hold us in their grip.

Living from pain

When pain is inevitable, eventually the realization comes that there's no other option than to learn to live with the long-term pain. For those who are unfamiliar with this predicament, from their own experience, it sounds easy, and supposedly well-meaning, to say so. But for those who suffer serious pain, it is still a hard blow. One cannot just fit pain, easily, into one's daily routine.

As a spiritual caregiver, I speak to many elderly people, every week, who are getting a little bit used to the idea that pain has become a part of them. Someone recently said: "This is me." In his experience, pain had become part of his personality. It is there, it does not go away, at least not like it used to. The pain remains a permanent shadow, but where there is shadow, there is light somewhere, a night and a day.

Miraculously, some people with pain develop a deeper self-awareness. There are different types of pain. A very old woman noted the following: "My greatest pain is not the physical but the mental," and "There is not a medicine for every pain." She was referring to the early death of her daughter, who came to visit her every other day and was her support and confidante.

Pain usually has a certain influence on the experience of happiness. People can experience this quite variously. Years ago, I spoke to the youngest resident in a nursing home. He had just turned 61. When I asked how he was doing, he gave the following nuanced answer: "I am not doing well, but I am happy." A few weeks later he died. I have never forgotten his statement. It taught me that suffering and life cannot be captured by standard and conventional ideas. Pain can be felt as a loss, as in losing yourself, but pain can also be experienced, strangely enough, in such a way as to bring you closer to yourself. It is therefore extremely important to listen very carefully, to take the time to let someone say what he or she wants to say, and to communicate very carefully. And not everything can and needs to be said right today.

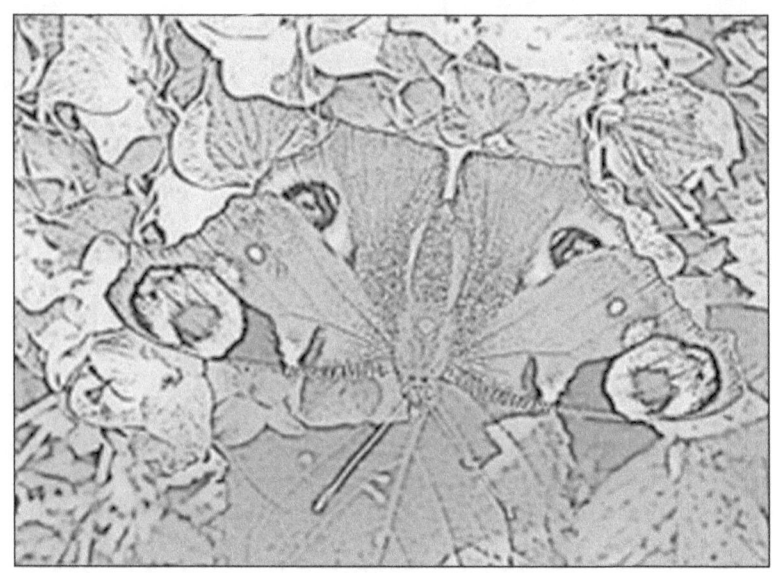

Flowers and those who love them

Do you remember that brilliant advertising slogan that we used to hear so often?

FLOWERS LOVE PEOPLE, GET THEM IN YOUR HOME!

This powerful and ironclad message, from the flower industry, made you feel warm. And who wasn't tempted to buy a beautiful bouquet for a loved one?

Flowers make you happy

With scents and colors of flowers you can surprise and make each other happy every day, whether you are ten or one-hundred years old. It is said that we shouldn't cover up anything in life. So, the gesture of a beautiful bouquet must be sincere.

Flowers and light

Anyone with the talent to cultivate a garden of flowers understands that flowers have nothing to hide. If they look beautiful and fresh, they are in fertile soil, as the gardener can tell, with the right amount of sunlight. Unseen, the light contributes to the wonder of the flowers.

One evening last spring, while the days were very long, a pink glow of evening light came over the garden at about half past nine in the evening, almost like the light of the roses! These last rays of sun were reflected upon the stately cumulus clouds, sailing slowly along in the sky, like galleons when quacking geese return to their nest in V-formation, just before the bats hunt in the twilight.

In silence

In complete silence, the flowers close their petals, as softly as they open, again, in the morning by the first sun light. Flowers, plants, and trees grow and thrive in a divine silence, averse to human noise and commotion. Butterflies flutter in silence. The bumblebees and bees do their uninterrupted work. The ants under the garden tiles also make no sound. An inaudible inner voice tells them exactly what to do: to produce life, each in their own way, with a higher purpose, possibly, of displaying the artistry of the Creator.

Flowers and beauty

The flowers have an unprecedented beauty and splendor and the butterflies resemble flying flowers with all their rich color and shades.

It is a pity that the photo above, of the peacock butterfly on a hydrangea flower, is not printed in color—for you to appreciate the light blue flower, with green leaves in the background; and on top, the reddish-brown butterfly with its big blue eyes, quietly enjoying the nectar. The butterfly, instinctively, takes the pollen along to the other flowers.

Let's talk about love. There are many preliminaries, before we may enjoy the quiet, natural pleasure of our flower bouquet, brought from the florist, to delight our loved ones! Those who take the time to reflect give flowers with even more affection.

Flowers and Transience

In Israel, the land of the Bible, some 2800 species of flower have been discovered, yet only the rose and the lily are mentioned by name. With its many, highly diverse landscapes, from the deserts of the South to the coastal areas of the West, and the mountains of Lebanon in the North, flowers grow everywhere in every season, and they are specific to the region in question.

Unsurprisingly, the flower is a symbol of beauty, in general, but there is much more. Love and the joy of life also contribute to the symbolic value of flowers. Yes, earthly beauty is transient. Flowers once picked are doomed to die quickly, since they've been taken from the earth, and they last at most a few days in water. And then they disappear into the bin, or, if they are lucky, onto the compost heap. The short-lived beauty of the flower is the symbol of earthly transience, at the same time, expressed vividly in the Bible:

> As for mortals, their days are like grass;
>   they flourish like a flower of the field;
> for the wind passes over it, and it is gone,
>   and its place knows it no more.   Psalm 103:15-16

Lasting value

It is sad but true. Flowers wither and fade, but clever salesmen have found a solution. Nowadays we are blessed, so to speak, with plastic flowers, Christmas trees, and other plants. They are eagerly bought with plastic money. In the spring, anything that can fly is still attracted to the eye-catching splendor, but the insects with their sharp sense of smell quickly notice that something is wrong. "This is fake news, this is surely man again who wants to emulate the Creator," they seem to complain. "Nothing more than plastic joy!" Then painters will know better, for they still recognize the beauty worth painting in the faded flowers.

The aging person may sooner or later experience himself as a withered bunch of flowers. "What will the end of life be like? Growing old is beautiful, but being old less so."

Those who are receptive to it may keep the idea and the Word of the Creator within themselves as a precious jewel:

> The grass withers, the flower fades;
> but the word of our God will stand forever.
> Isaiah 40:8

Cherish good memories because they are eternal, just like God's Word!

Loneliness

Loneliness is annoying, gnawing, and uncomfortable, just like all experiences of loss. Let me put it this way.

For example, people sometimes say, almost casually, that they were once divorced. Someone I spoke to suddenly felt a distance from everyone—from the family, in the first place, but also relatives, friends, and even colleagues. Loneliness can be accompanied by strong shame. The first reaction, in the case of a divorce, is to save whatever can be saved, out of a survival instinct, and a hope (usually in vain) for a new start to the marriage: "Although I detested the idea of divorce, I still had to learn to live with it by continuing to get the best out of myself. I encouraged myself by resolving to do something every day that would give me and others joy." And that seemed to help this person somewhat. It freed the person from endless, and limitless, brooding, lasting into the middle of the night.

Apparently, one must go ahead by standing up, possibly strengthened by prayer and faith, and also by many people around you. Yes, they suddenly appear to be there. People try to offer comfort, albeit not always in the right style. A good friend is precious.

Lonely among many

If you no longer live independently, you may live in a large house with many fellow residents. I say 'fellow residents', but not everyone experiences fellow feeling. All sorts of feelings may be present in a jumble, one may need to be careful not to say the wrong thing.

Some say that they feel lonely because they miss people of the same age, people with whom to talk about familiar topics. Where can you find fellow residents with whom you click a bit?

An exceptionally welcome topic at the table, or over coffee, are our shortcomings and handicaps. It goes without saying that you should also share your feelings about inconveniences. Don't keep your heart in a dark place. It does not stir up gratitude when shortcomings are repeated, as if there is nothing better to talk about. Then, the topic is depressing. Keep a good balance in conversation and a pleasant atmosphere.

Stay positive

Back to meeting people with whom you can have a good conversation, it's a cliché of sorts, but to keep thinking and feeling positive is the basis for happiness. Even if you slept badly, and you feel like trash, think just then:

"How can I make someone else happy on this new day?"

"Those who do good, will receive good" says the proverb. This is a beautiful and rich thought, and it's edifying. And if one person fails to appreciate your joyful dedication, then there are countless others who will be happy and grateful, in the morning or the afternoon, or perhaps not until the evening, and they will give you a sweet wink in return. Then, your own loneliness may subside.

Loneliness and faith

For Christian believers, it could be an inspiration to realize that Jesus experienced much brokenness in His earthly life: disregard, misunderstanding, betrayal from His close circle, abuse, and ultimately death on the cross. Even for Him, this led to a deep and intense feeling of abandonment, by other people, but especially God, in His dying hour. An angel came to strengthen Him on the evening before His death.

Feeling abandoned is the most striking characterization of loneliness. The abandonment that Jesus felt on the cross was extreme: He had not expected to feel abandoned especially by the Father:

> My God, My God, why have You forsaken me?
>
> Psalm 22:1 / Matthew 27:46

This was His last word, according to Matthew, but according to the evangelist Luke, His last words were:

> Father, into your hands I commend my spirit.
>
> Luke 23:46 (see also Psalm 31:5)

Both exclamations are citations from the Psalms. And that shows that a prayer at the moment of death always makes sense. The great Indian freedom fighter Mahatma Gandhi (1869-1948) had trained himself to die in this way, that is, while praying. When he was murdered in a crowd with three shots by a fanatical Hindu, who thought that Gandhi was too conciliatory towards Muslims, his last words were "Hai Ram," "O God." And so the dying person dedicates his entire life to God.

The feeling of brokenness

The brokenness and abandonment that Jesus experienced is depicted in our church services by the breaking of the bread, as Jesus himself did so often: at the multiplication of the loaves, during the Last Supper and after the Resurrection. Think of the remarkable story of the two disciples on the way to Emmaus, the day after the crucifixion of Jesus:

> So he went in to stay with them. When he was at the table with them, he took bread, blessed and broke it, and gave it to them. Then their eyes were opened, and they rec-

ognized him; and he vanished from their sight. They said to each other, "Were not our hearts burning within us while he was talking to us on the road, while he was opening the scriptures to us?" Luke 24:29b-32

The broken bread is a longing for the one bread. Where brokenness has arisen in people's lives, the bread broken by Jesus points to a deeper inner wholeness, symbolized by the one undivided bread.

Sometimes people say that they have definitely broken with others. Jesus breaks the bread so that unity arises: everyone eats from the one shared bread, which precisely, as broken bread, becomes a symbol of community, where loneliness is abolished, although not everyone will experience that in this way.

Community

In the Gospel of John, Jesus says of himself:

I am the bread of life. John 6:35

On the road to Emmaus with the disciples, in the gospel, the Bread of Life breaks itself, as He did at the Sea of Galilee for thousands, and there was still bread left for everyone, for us, who came after Him. And that is why our mothers used to scratch a cross in the bread before it was cut. After all, the one bread is for the whole family, not just for the one with the greatest hunger.

By breaking the bread and giving Himself as broken bread, the Lord breaks our loneliness. The pieces of broken bread are nourishing for those who receive them. The image of the broken bread is indeed the image of a lost unity, but that unity is coming back! For loneliness becomes community and communion, as the Apostle Paul says:

> The cup of blessing that we bless, is it not a sharing in the blood of Christ? The bread that we break, is it not a sharing in the body of Christ?
> 17 Because there is one bread, we who are many are one body, for we all partake of the one bread. 1 Corinthians 10:16-17

And behold: the brokenness of loneliness is, in a wonderful way, the fertile soil for the final perspective of life: namely, that of a definitive communion in and with God: God-with-us, Immanuel.

What do you live for?

Once, in one of my former parishes, a walking tour was announced for Lent. The plan was to publish a booklet with themes along the way. I was also asked to fill a page for that day. Since in past centuries, most people walked and filled many of their steps with their own thoughts, the theme, "What do you live for?" seemed very appropriate, or, "Why are you going for a walk?" The question of course also arises, "What did you live for in the past?", and "What was your motivation in life?" Hopefully, this is material for nice conversations!

Seeing life as a walk

In March, we set off. Together, from one church to another. It is not to be a silent march to commemorate someone or the Silent Procession in Amsterdam, but simply a walk as a conversation to meet others, around the question, "What do you live for?" for Lent, the time of reflection, prayer, and fasting in preparation for the Easter celebration.

"What do you live for?" People usually answer: 'family', 'work', 'holiday', in short, the people and activities that receive daily attention. But... as the walk goes further, beyond the boundaries of our own village, other answers come to the surface. Answers from the deeper layer of life, perhaps. Then, it turns out that the question, "What do you live for?" is a question that regularly occupies our minds, unconsciously, even though we do not always talk about it.

The longer the walk, the closer the walker gets to himself or herself and hopefully to his or her fellow walkers. That is how the stories of long-distance walkers sound, such as those of the pilgrims to Santiago de Compostella, for example. By the way, for how many kilometers has Jesus been without travelling with His disciples?

Is it surprising that walking is compared in the Bible to how people live? We still know the expression 'walk of life'. Then we are not talking about the ability to use up kilometers during the Four Days Marches in Nijmegen. It is about someone's life story and especially about their moral behavior. The 'walk of life' tells of the whole person that I am. And hence the question, "What do you actually live for?" is equal to the question, "Who are you actually?" If you go a little deeper, these questions often occupy our minds, but we still have difficulty finding an answer to them. We grope in the dark in search of an answer, which is hidden somewhere deep in our hearts.

In our search, the Bible comes to our aid by turning the question around. God asks Adam, the first human being, a question:

> Where are you? Genesis 3:9

This makes it the very first question that God asks when someone hides in his own shame. In the Gospel of John, too, the very first thing Jesus asks you as a disciple is:

> What are you looking for? John 1:38

That great God, who made heaven and earth, does not begin with a wise lesson or a profound thought, but with a direct question: "You, man, where are you in your life? What are you looking for? What do you desire?" The Bible is God's living Word, which goes through the centuries like a walking island, surrounded by the storms of every age. It is the Eternal, our God himself, who walks with us. The concept of walking is heavily loaded in the Bible. For example, it was said about the death of Enoch, one of Noah's ancestors:

> Enoch walked with God; then he was no more, because God took him. Genesis 5:24

Whoever lives completely in God will never die. This person is preserved in God. Ultimately, we humans may walk before God's Countenance in the divine Light. Since the time of Adam, to hide from God makes little sense, because God goes looking for you like a shepherd, as a parent does when a child fails to come home in the evening. This is also as Jesus Himself actively does when He heals the man born blind, who is then expelled from his own community, as the Gospel says:

> Jesus heard that they had driven him out, and when he found him, he said, "Do you believe in the Son of Man?" John 9:35

Thank God, we will never be separated from the heavenly Father, no matter what happens to us, because God seeks us out and visits us. Therefore, here's a promise in strong biblical terms, so that you know that you are in good company when you walk together:

> And I will walk among you, and will be your God, and you shall be my people. Leviticus 26:12

What do you live for? This remains a question to ask yourself daily.

Spring, Lent and Easter

Every major celebration has a preparation period. Anyone who has ever celebrated an anniversary with the entire family and one's circle of friends knows what has preceded. Such preparation is a time of thinking carefully and forgetting nothing;

there's much consultation and occasional irritations. Fortunately, preparing for a celebration is mainly a time of fun and anticipation of fun.

Easter has its preparation period that closely follows on from winter. After all, in winter people have built up fat reserves against the cold, and by dieting or fasting during Lent, we lose the excess or surplus kilos and pounds. This time of natural fasting is used in the churches to fast not only physically but also spiritually.

Fasting in a spiritual sense is a broad concept; it's the choice for a long-term sober lifestyle, and keeping its purpose in mind, a time for a stronger focus on who the human being is in relation to God. In this way, fasting creates a spiritual water spring in the life of faith, a new physical-spiritual balance.

Incidentally, the Old English word for 'fasting' is 'to lent'. The verb "to lent' comes from 'the lengthening of the days in the spring', so the time in which the days lengthen happens in the spring. People then prepare for Easter and fast for forty days, as Jesus did in the desert after His baptism in the Jordan by John the Baptist.

Fasting is not a goal in itself but a form of prayer. Throughout the centuries, Holy Scripture has emphasized the need to support fasting by prayer. Both reinforce each other: fasting is praying with the body. And praying is like fasting through the spirit. By praying, one enters the spiritual world of the Divine. Just as God seeks out man, the praying person no longer seeks himself but God. Love for God makes love for one's fellows more profound. Fellow human beings are vital to faith, especially during fasting.
And so, during the weeks of the Great Lent, preceding Easter, the Orthodox Churches pray the following fasting prayer by someone we have already

encountered, namely the Church Father Ephrem the Syrian (+ 373 in Edessa):

O Lord and Master of my life!
Take from me the spirit of sloth,
faint-heartedness, lust for power and idle talk.
But give rather the spirit of chasity,
humility, patience and love to Thy servant.
Yes, Lord and King!
Grant me to see my own errors
and not to judge my brother;
For Thou art blessed unto ages and ages. Amen[4]

Easter

Easter is originally the Jewish thanksgiving for the spring harvest. In the past, everything depended on a good harvest, whether your family had enough to eat for the next few months or hardly anything. Our ancestors knew that very well and perhaps you yourself still have clear memories of it.

When new life announces itself, there is certainly great joy, and even a joy greater than we can comprehend. This joy transcends us, just as life itself can do and thus become intangible: we have it, but it seems to elude us just as easily. Nature around us is of a non-human order. Let us at least agree on that. It is an order that humans manage but do not own.

The spring festival of Easter, the celebration of the Resurrection of Christ, is about the truth of our human life: who we are in the whole of God's creation.

---

4 From: Alexander Schmemann, Great Lent – Journey to Pascha St.Vladimir's Seminary Press, 575 Scarsdale Road, Crestwood, NY 10707; 1-800-204-2665 www.svs.com - 1969 / ISBN 978-0-913839-04-0, p.34)

New life is exuberantly celebrated in the Easter Vigil on Easter Saturday evening: new fire, new light, and new baptismal water are blessed, and everything is a sign of the Risen Lord, Who will rise from the grave this night.

In doing so, He opens wide the doors of the prison of our temporary existence. You are a free person again! You may leave the cell of your earthly life behind you, you may walk the path of your new life in Christ, as the Apostle Paul so beautifully puts it:

> If we have died with Christ, we believe that we will also live with him. Romans 6:8

The full moon

Have you ever noticed that there is always a full moon in the sky at or around Easter? You might wonder if that is a coincidence. It is no coincidence at all. Easter in the western Church was planned in such a way as to fall, every year, on the Sunday after the first full spring moon. The first full moon in spring thus became the symbol of the new light of life. And the Christians saw in the light a reference to the Resurrection of Jesus from the grave. The first Christians still lived according to their Jewish traditions. The Jewish calendar takes the course of the moon as the benchmark for the whole of life. Is it surprising that the moon is contained in our word 'month'? No, this is actually very logical. The influence of the moon on the earth is greater than we usually suspect. The moon exerts its influence with an ebb and flow. This cosmic consciousness transmits a grateful knowledge that we are part of an unspeakably great mystery.

A holy atmosphere

We have come into the atmosphere of a new, ever-renewing life, into a holy atmosphere, that transcends man. The word holy will frighten many people. However, a holy atmosphere means an environment where the human becomes whole again, healed, because whole and holy are like brother and sister. This is the atmosphere where we as human beings come into our own again in the full sense of the word, in other words, justice is done. We are sanctified and healed not by our own behavior and good will, but by the wholeness of the transcendent Divine. It is the Holiness of God that makes us holy.

The Easter egg

We may become perfect, like the perfect shape of the egg, another important Easter symbol of new life. Easter as a church liturgical celebration is a holy space that the human may enter. It is a foretaste of the new Life, to which we are ultimately destined.

The icon of Easter

In the Christian East, icons have traditionally been painted images, for the Liturgy, of Christ and the saints. The actual painting is preceded by an intensive process of preparation. Paint is made by mixing egg yolk with the dyes of flowers or other raw materials from nature. So people consciously draw on what nature provides.

In the Christian East, each feast day has its own icon, which is venerated in the Church on that day. At Easter, the icon of the Resurrection of Jesus from the dead is of course central. The icon visually recalls Jesus's resurrection, the story of which is read at the Easter celebration. Jesus is depicted, risen from the grave—He, Who has risen and then descended into hell, as the old faith confession puts it. In the Easter icon, the Risen Lord pulls Adam and Eve, the first human beings, up from their grave. Like Adam and Eve, every person is destined, in principle, to be freed from sin and death.

Easter and afterward

Easter is both the end of a period, the forty-day season of Lent, and a new beginning, that of the seven weeks of Pentecost, the second Jewish harvest festival. A sharp distinction is often made between the earthly life of Jesus and His Ascension with the Father in Heaven. But such a line of demarcation is not correct. During His earthly life, Jesus was already very strongly connected to Heaven, and now that He has ascended to Heaven, He is even more connected to the earth than he was during His earthly life:

> I will not leave you orphaned; I am coming to you. John 14:18

He said that just before His death. These were His very last words:

> And remember, I am with you always, to the end of the age. Matt 28:20

This is the conclusion of the Gospel of Matthew, just before the Risen Lord ascends into heaven.

Wind – Water – Light

Speaking of the play of wind and water, years ago we were on holiday in Croatia. We had found a beautiful place on the Adriatic Sea. It soon became apparent that the wind and water were not always harmonious, for we arrived at our destination in a heavy storm, with grey skies, cold, and downpours. That day seemed to be the harbinger of a holiday that risked falling into the water, but in the course of the evening, the air began to clear, as we say.

The word "clear" expresses light, which makes clear. Early the next morning, there was not a cloud in the sky. A clear blue sky smiled at us, and the

Croatian sun did what the Dutch tourist expects, namely provide nice warm weather. The sea had become as still and blue as the sky itself. And so wind, water, and light alternated daily.

Clearing Up

I took a photo of exactly the same view every day and each photo showed a completely different image of the landscape. Thus, I became aware that light participates in the play of wind and water. When wind, water and sunlight are attuned to one another to our liking, we speak of clearings.

In the past, the verb 'clear' was used professionally with the meaning of having been completed (i.e. "The job is cleared"). But spiritually, clarity also happens when one makes a clear statement. That also seems to be true in the Bible.

At home in infinity

In the very first Bible verses, we read that "the Spirit of God was brought over the waters." The Spirit blows as the breath of God. It is precisely then that God declares: "Let there be Light!" At that moment, there is Light, divine Light, indeed before the luminaries have been created. Note, the statement is in the present tense! The Spirit and the Light: they go together, even today. I felt that connection very clearly there on the Adriatic Sea!

Speaking of the purity of the country: in Limburg they certainly rightly sing: "How clean is our Limburg," but as a man from the coast, I secretly think:

There is nothing better than the wild simplicity of the beach. There you can feel sand, sea, and water with your bare feet. And that feels like you are walking on holy ground, as if you are walking on the light, When you go to the beach, you don't have to take anything with you. You just sit and feel the infinity all around.
Once, I realized on the beach that our human spirit feels completely at home in this infinity. The spirit comes home to God's infinity! You don't have to be or do anything; you only have to feel one with the sand, water, wind, and light. In this way, you will feel clear and bright, and the atmosphere brings you toward the Spirit of God, as Jesus describes, which blows through us:

> Do not be astonished that I said to you, "You must be born from above." The wind blows where it chooses, and you hear the sound of it, but you do not know where it comes from or where it goes. So it is with everyone who is born of the Spirit. John 3:7-8

A fresh start every morning

This new birth is like being created anew, and coming back to life, "being born of the Spirit." God always starts something new in you, every morning. Every morning there is a fresh start in store for you. With bare feet, you stand up, you rise, on the holy ground of your own life story.

The wind starts to flow like water and the water starts to blow like the wind. Everything clears and becomes bright in you. A new day, that never existed before, has dawned.

'Our mother'

When I speak of mother, what image or thought comes to mind? There is a good chance that you immediately think of 'my mother', 'our mother', as they say in Brabant.

Many older people return to their youth a little and think more often about who and what their own parents were like:

"My mother was always..."
"My mother sometimes said..."
"My mother was good at..."
"Even at a later age my mother..."
"I still remember well that she..."
"My father and mother..."
"When she was already very ill..."

"On the day she died..."
Everyone colors the image "my mother" very personally with their own feelings. For example, if your family had seven children in the past, each child will have different memories. For example, while involved in preparing a funeral, I once experienced that the eldest son was much more critical (and negative) about their deceased mother than the youngest. Things came up that they had never really talked about. The difference in opinion almost became a problem, before the funeral, since they disagreed as to how they wanted to commemorate their mother.

My mother and I

Then comes the beautiful question: What was the very first memory of your mother? What do you remember from the time when you were very young?

I'll let you think for a moment and speak out of turn. When I was five, my mother, like so many women, used to sew at home, a lot, on that old Singer, which was meant for my two sisters. I used to ask, with curiosity, whether she could make something for me. No sooner said than it would be done, in no time. She made a beautiful sky-blue shirt for me. And so, I wore something of my mother! I was very proud of it; that goes without saying.

So your very first memory of your mother...I hope for you that it is a dear memory. If that is indeed the case, you will have learned, and absorbed, a great deal from your mother.

It also happens, sadly, that people may have various and even bad experiences. These experiences can be too painful for words; such as that of being unwanted, neglected, or ignored, to the point of abuse and violence. Children might grow up in a very unsafe atmosphere. Unimaginable, but unfortunately, this used to happen and it still happens too often.

Your childhood

As you grew up in childhood, you realized, little by little, that your parents remained still the children of their parents. They told you their experiences of childhood and how different life was in their time.

Not long ago, the concept of the generation gap was introduced. This was probably felt more strongly in the post-war years. The entire society seemed incomparable to what came before. Because of all the changes, people came to stand quite opposite to each other. But still, there was (generally) no splitting up. Marriages were maintained for the sake of the children or to uphold the family honor, although many people actually wanted to divorce.

At the same time, many married people agreed that their married life was good and warm, simply. They got energy and strength from it. After all, a little give and take does no harm. Many older people look back with gratitude and nostalgia on their marriages, sometimes of 60 years or more. Their thick photo albums have well-thumbed pages, having been turned over countless times.

Your parental home

A symbol of a close and communal life is surely the parental home, where parents may have continued to live during their entire lives. This home is a world that was also your own, and in which good relationships were maintained. The large families of the past were usually very pleasant, despite the fact that people did not always have much money.

To return to the childhood environment makes it easier to recall memories. I know that from experience. When I visited my father in The Hague, the house was exactly as it was in my youth in every particular. I could even move back into my attic room, in that stately mansion, near the Peace Palace.

Becoming a mother or father yourself

Another moment when your youth returns is when you become a parent. To have children cannot be accomplished just by a snap of the fingers, however. To have children is to receive a gift. For the woman, motherhood is intense, emotionally and physically, and an entirely different experience from fatherhood, for her husband.

Mother's Day

Halfway through May, all eyes turn to the mother. For some, the holiday is very beautiful and unforgettable, while others would rather not dwell on it. When you haven't had children of your own, it can be painful to hear everyone talking about their children and grandchildren. You're not a mother and it may sting that they are mothers. Mother's Day can also be difficult if your relationship with your mother has been disrupted. But by reconciling with your fate, you may learn about your personal destiny.

To have children means a new life phase, giving the young mother reason to ask her own mother how motherhood used to be in her time. A brand new grandma loves to be asked about the past. What a lot of charming topics between the grandmother and mother, which makes the husband wonder what he's really good for. Well, he will soon learn to enjoy his new identity as a young father too.

In this regard, here's a brief anecdote from my own memoirs when I had just become a father. For weeks my wife had practiced the 'press' in her pregnancy course. At home, she would tell me all about it. When I, as a young father, went to register our daughter at the Almere City Hall after the birth, I passed the 'press room' right in front of the population counter. I had to switch gears for a moment. That press room was probably slightly different!

Bond with your mother

To be honest, the bond with your father is very different from that with your mother. It is actually not so easy to explain, but it feels different. Undoubtedly, that mysterious 'maternal intuition' is at play. You could hide from your father, occasionally, or act in secret. He would be far too busy to notice. But your mother...that good person really seemed to sense it all and to see right through you. Call it a supernatural gift given to women. She only had to look at you and you knew: "She's figured it out again!" Of course, a mother hen who watches over her chicks by fluffing up her feathers when danger looms does make you feel safe. But as a toddler, you weren't always ready for her unsolicited vigilance.

Anyone who later becomes a mother or father themselves will have fondly reminisced about childhood with Grandpa and Grandma. The young offspring, in turn, will enjoy such memories when their ears are big enough. By the time they are teenagers, a new awareness comes: "Mom, Dad, tell me about the past again." So the generation gap loses its sharp edge, hopefully—too bad, not always. The elderly person places all such recollections in their proper perspective and preserves what's worth cherishing.

What is painful

As I mentioned, many of you either could not have children, sadly, when you wanted to, or you have had children but they've already died before you, in one way or another. This is the inevitable fate of those who reach old age: the chance that their own children will die is extremely painful, especially if it is an only child. Friends and acquaintaces will die, too, of course, but the loss of a child inflicts the deepest wounds. Hopefully, with each new setback, people will find places and ways to honor the lost child, as well as other loved ones. Put it this way: one dies a little bit with them.

No more contact

Another kind of dying happens when parents and children are estranged. They no longer desire mutual contact. Beyond the defeat of hope, life takes here an extra hard turn. Hopefully, people will keep the door ajar, in the recesses of their hearts, awaiting a mutual and auspicious reconciliation; it may happen despite all, even if it arrives on the last day of life, or at the hour of death. Reconciliation is comforting and constructive for all parties.

Normally, our mothers and fathers are well worth remembering. They have given us birth, shaped us, cared for us, listened to us, and given us good advice. They've always been there when we've needed them. They have kept us in mind and often remembered us in their prayers before the face of the Heavenly Father. They've been our housemates and fellow travelers, sharing our joys and sorrows. They've been grumpy, sometimes, and headstrong in their old age, but they've remained our Mam and miene Pap in Brabant and Limburg. And in Frisian, North Holland, The Hague or Zeeland or Suriname, these terms of endearment sound just as intense and just as beautiful.

So, give tribute to them, our parents, who have loved us! What they've given us, we in turn have been able to give them: loving attention and care. They've taught us well. The life that has been received and then passed on; the love that has come to true fruition. Where our upbringing may have gone wrong, they've been forgiven.

Was everything created?

Is the earth and the entire universe the work of a Divine Creator or did it simply come into being from a Big Bang? About this subject, it is not easy to reach agreement, but nevertheless it stimulates a good conversation. Let us explore this theme in more detail.

The starry sky

Every now and then, there are new photos, in the media, and articles about the sun, planets, or galaxies. Never before have we witnessed such beautiful and detailed images. The photos are absolutely fascinating. Unbelievable, that this beauty is all around. Light that comes from billions of light years away. You feel small and insignificant. It is clear that as humans we have not lost our sense of wonder.

Our distant ancestors were probably much more interested in the stars and the universe than we modern people. In an era without electricity or artificial light, it must have been pitch black on the streets at night, apart from street lamps holding candles. In a cloudless sky, you could undoubtedly marvel at the stars. During the war, at night, when the streets had to remain shrouded in darkness, the stars were comforting and encouraging. The occupying country could not possibly forbid people to look up at the sky. They were free to behold the greatness of the universe, in amazement, as the Psalmist did:

> What are human beings that you are mindful of them,
> mortals that you care for them?
> Yet you have made them a little lower than God,
> and crowned them with glory and honor.
> Psalm 8:4-5

The human being in balance with the environment

Nowadays, it might be unsafe to be outside during the evening and at night, but in the past the experience was more intense, with wild animals likely to be all around you: rats in cities and wolves in the countryside. And don't forget owls and bats! "Nighttime is for vermin" is a proverb for a reason—for burglars and bombers. And on top of that, people used to be terrified of devils, demons, and witches, who all become active at night. There used to be, indeed, all the difference between day and night. In the past, the day was spent working and the night given for sleeping or to pray, as Jesus did. The monks imitate Him, getting up at 4:00 in the morning for their first communal prayer. They get up to sanctify the night.

The rhythm of day and night determines the life of human beings as we are (created) to be. I put "created" in brackets, because not everyone believes that our earth was (or would be) created. What we can perhaps agree upon is that the entire universe, including the earth, was there long before we were born.

Sooner or later, a child is amazed by the world of animals, plants, insects, flowers, and, as he grows older, by being human itself. The more we keep this wonder alive, the more respect we will have for our living environment. For the environment will give us energy and wisdom. Nature is the best school.

A human-friendly creation

It is amazing that our natural environment is extremely human friendly. There is air to breathe, water to drink, fruit on the trees, grain with which to bake bread, a sun that gives light and warmth, and even flowers to pick, as gifts and tokens of friendship. In principle, all for free!
It is quite an achievement for people to land on the moon and walk around in space suits, but on earth, we do not need space suits, unless you go deep-sea diving. The entire earth is our only space suit. We

are becoming increasingly aware of this. It is up to mankind not to disturb the sophisticated earthly balance, but to live in harmony with it.

Poets, writers, and painters have always been inspired by nature. The light, the colors, and the beauty of everything always prove overwhelming. M. Vasalis expresses this aptly in her poem below (1909 – 1998):

The Donkey

*In the short, blue twilight I took
a little walk. The ground was red,
cracked-dry.
The air was thin and terribly high, and blue
thistles stiff and capricious
rustled eagerly and reluctantly.*

*Grazing quietly next to a gray rock I suddenly saw
a young donkey on high legs;
his ears seemed transparent, his face was
proud.*

*His long, amber eyes shone and impartial
was his gaze.
And after a short, sharp fright
I froze in amazement,
Or could it have been reverence
for this beautiful, unblemished animal, with which
I slowly continued?*

*A painful memory:
I used to be like that too.
That coolness and gentleness,
unburdened seriousness and dreaminess,
oh if I could regain that once more,
if I could start again once more.*[5]

---

5 M. Vasalis, Parks and Deserts (1983). M.Vasalis pseudonym of Margaretha Drooglever Fortuyn-Leenmans. Parken en woestijnen: gedichten / M. Vasalis. - Groningen: Wolters-Noordhoff, 1993. - 27 p.; 20 cm. - (Gro-

Creation or not?

Now the question is whether we, the earth, and the entire universe were brought to life by a higher power. Let's place some figures in a row: according to science, the earth is supposedly 4.5 billion years old, while the Milky Way has existed for about 13 billion years. Science collects all kinds of data, starts calculating, and then derives conclusions without apparent bias or personal feeling.

However, humans have not only the ability to think and calculate. Their consciousness can make them feel and move them emotionally. Humans even have a remarkable ability to rise above themselves. Humans create beautiful music, art, architecture, and eye-catching cities. You have probably been able to admire all of this during cultural visits or on vacation.

There must be something!

Even more important is that humans can step over their own shadow through courage, love, and forgiveness. So humans have many more abilities than just arithmetic skills. People have made use of these special abilities for centuries. They suspect, "There must be something more."

Nowadays they call that *somethingism*.

---

te lijsters, ISSN 0925-4617; 199306) Licentie-uitg. van: Amsterdam: Van Oorschot. - Oorspr. uitg.: Rijswijk: Stols, 1940. - (Helikon; jrg. 10, no. 10). ISBN 90-01-54796-6 ISBN 90-01-54790-7, p.18. Translated by Guram Kochi MSc

Back to the question of whether everything that exists has been created. Of course, it is the same question, whether or not there God exists as Creator. This all revolves around the simple question: "Is it a coincidence that everything exists or not?"

Everything is a coincidence

Yes, it is a coincidence, says one group of scientists. We can establish that the universe came into being a long time ago, with the Big Bang, and has developed very slowly into what it is today. The idea of an the evolution of species, presented by Charles Darwin in 1859, fits in very well with that account.

Everything is not a coincidence

No, it is precisely not a coincidence, says the other group of scientists, who claim: Evolution can indeed be established, but it does not explain the clear blueprint underlying evolution. Is it a coincidence that humans, and many animals, are built according to a pattern? Senses, organs and limbs have similar kinds of body structure. So, the human being seems to have been planned by an architect, a higher intellect. This group of scientists posit the so-called Intelligent Design theory.

Look carefully!

Incidentally, for Buddhists, questions about the existence of god(s) or the origins of things are not at all interesting. For them, there is no beginning or end. What matters is how we look at what's around us, from which perspective, and in particular, how we deal with the suffering experienced by all humans. So, it is important to look, at least, beyond our noses.

Creation as a widespread idea

The idea that God, as the highest power, created all that exists comes not only from the Judeo-Christian and Islamic traditions. Almost all indigenous peoples have their own creation story. For centuries, those peoples have told their children, from generation to generation, about the origins of their own tribe, from where they came, and how they came into being. Similarly, they asked, "Who are we and what is our mission in this life?" For the primordial human, living in nature, dreams and visions are of great importance. They're an important part of experience in the world. From this perspective, people become convinced that a higher power has set everything into motion. Nature was not created by human hands alone.

We modern people, with all our technical knowledge, search less for the meaning of our dreams. But we know that while humans can do much, they can't do everything. It is quite an achievement if we manage to live in peace with one another, here on earth, and if we distribute our wealth equally.

Contact with the Higher Power

The idea that we've been created is widespread in many cultures, which shows that humans are generally religious and spiritual beings. The human being draws on sources that are beyond our understanding.

Man's ability to communicate even enables him to come into contact with the Higher Power. Believers do this in and through prayer. Others, who do not believe in a personal God, such as Buddhists, meditate on the mystery of being human in this world. The goal of this is as the monk above explained: "to see the ground of everything" and gain insight. Ancient Greek and Roman philosophers did exactly the same thing.

The book of Job on creation

In the broad stream of human thought, the Bible presents all as having been created by God. The biblical story of creation is the basis for all its other stories. The Psalms in particular praise the greatness of creation, and the book of Job does not mince words. Here, God manifests Himself emphatically as the Creator when Job calls God to account.

Job was a rich man, possessed of everything his heart desired; he was a successful entrepreneur, we might say. The story tell us at the start: "He was the richest man in the East." Above all, Job was a man of faith. He was aware that he owed everything to God.

Then Satan asks God for permission to test Job. He is given permission, but on the condition that Job himself as a person is not harmed. Everything that Job has built up is then knocked out of his hands. His friends start discussing his problems with him, while inquiring about the strength of his faith, and eventually Job reproaches God. Angry and disappointed, he nevertheless keeps returning to God. He remains convinced that God hears him. He desires, repeatedly, to pray. Then a text follows that captures the actual message of the book. God pours out speeches, for many chapters, after Job has expressed his doubts. In the wind and storm, it says, God will give Job His answer. And God starts with a penetrating question:

> Where were you when I laid the foundation of the earth?
> Tell me, if you have understanding. Job 38:4

Here, the text captures the style of the Bible with its extremely rich language. From chapter 38 to 41, God subtly explains in every possible way Who He is as Creator. The animals, plants, sun, moon, and even the galaxies are included in the smallest details. In the meanwhile, Job only gets to speak briefly. He is already very impressed, but God thunders on for two more chapters. Wonderful to read, what a rich use of language! And then, finally, we are at the end of chapter 41, God seems to have finished raging, and then the text reads, with that characteristic biblical candor, like the calm after a storm:

> Then Job answered the Lord:
> 2 'I know that you can do all things,
> and that no purpose of yours can be thwarted.
> 3 "Who is this that hides counsel without knowledge?"
> Therefore I have uttered what I did not understand,

> things too wonderful for me, which I did not know.
> 4 "Hear, and I will speak;
> I will question you, and you declare to me."
> 5 I had heard of you by the hearing of the ear,
> but now my eye sees you;
> 6 therefore I despise myself,
> and repent in dust and ashes.' Job 42:1-6

How topical these words sound! The book of Job ends with a brotherly reconciliation between the Creator and his creature. And then all is well that ends well:

> The Lord blessed the latter days of Job more than his beginning; and he had fourteen thousand sheep, six thousand camels, a thousand yoke of oxen, and a thousand donkeys. Job 42:12

> After this Job lived for one hundred and forty years, and saw his children, and his children's children, four generations. Job 42:16

Creation or not?

Whether or not the human being lives in a world created by God will always concern us. As long as we humans live on earth, and do not know the answer one hundred percent, we would at least do well to maintain the earth and pass it along intact to all who are yet to be born.

Mary, the Mother of the Lord

Mary, as the mother of Jesus, is consistently called the 'mother of the Lord' in the New Testament. In this sense, she is the 'Mother of the Church' because of the last words of Jesus at the hour of His death, as expressed in the Gospel of John:

> And that is what the soldiers did.
> Meanwhile, standing near the cross of Jesus were his mother, and his mother's sister, Mary the wife of Clopas, and Mary Magdalene.
> 26 When Jesus saw his mother and the disciple whom he loved standing beside her,

he said to his mother, "Woman, here is your son."
27 Then he said to the disciple, "Here is your mother." And from that hour the disciple took her into his own home.
John 19:25-27

Behold your mother, behold the Church

The disciple whom Jesus loved much is John. He stands under the Cross as a representative of all future generations. You wouldn't think it, but these simple words, "Behold your mother!", say everything about us, because here we find the birth of the Church, the community that we are in Christ. It is a significant sign of hope that in that last, extremely painful hour of Jesus' death, Jesus emphatically turns His gaze to His mother, as the future 'Mother of the Church'. The gesture also indicates how strong His bond is with Mary, formulated in the present tense! The relationship of the Church with Mary creates a space and an atmosphere of prayer. Jesus Himself indicates that Mary can be included as a mother in prayer to the heavenly Father. So with much love and with great emphasis He says to the whole Church:

Behold your mother!

When His disciples asked Him earlier to teach them, and us, to pray, Jesus of course addressed His Father in heaven directly, but remarkably enough He addresses the Father as our common Father and not initially as His own Father:

Pray then in this way:
Our Father in heaven,
hallowed be your name. Matt 6:9

The invocation, 'Our Father,' sounds surprisingly new: with the Son of God, who also calls Himself the Son of Man, we are sons and daughters of the Father! Mary, as the one "full of grace," the "blessed among women" (Luke 1:28), is considered the first chosen one, because she was chosen to bear Jesus. The oldest churches have cherished this belief to this day. Mary will always retain a place of honor in the hearts of believers.

And yet, strictly speaking, nowhere in the New Testament does it say that we may pray to Mary and nowhere is Mary addressed as, for example, "Our Mother" as we say "Our Father." Jesus himself also seems to keep some distance from His mother, perhaps because Mary's motherhood cannot be compared to God's fatherhood. In the divine-human mystery of Jesus, there is always ambiguity: distance and proximity, knowing and not knowing. This tension keeps faith alive.

Veneration of Mary in a larger context

The Church has also borrowed veneration of Mary, within the framework of faith in Jesus, from the story of the wedding at Cana (John 2:1-12), in which Jesus changes the water into wine after a loving word from his mother. Mary is experienced as an advocate. The veneration of Mary often makes non-Catholics assume that Mary is given a divine status—certainly given her title Mother of God, that is to say, mother of the Son of God. The veneration of Mary, however, means that believers can come through Mary to Jesus and to God—as the Church has always taught. You have, as it were, the entrance (Jesus) with a portal (Mary).

Praying through the intercession of a saint

Praying to Mary is sometimes equated with praying to God by Catholics themselves. One risks opposition of one to the other. Other Christians note that praying to Mary is superfluous if you can pray directly to God, to Jesus, or the Holy Spirit. However, the Catholic Church does not say that we pray to Mary as a replacement for praying to God. The Church says that one prays through the intercession of Mary or of a certain saint. This is exactly the same as human intercession, where one asks, "Would you like to pray for me, because I really need it?" Then you pray for, and on behalf of, and with, that person. In evangelical churches, it is suggested often, "Shall we pray together?" because they hold that unanimous prayer accomplishes much.
Shouldering the burden together. The more souls, the more joy, we say proverbially. That ideal is exactly what Catholics invoke regarding Mary or other saints. The term 'Mary veneration' may place too much emphasis on Mary and therefore raise questions. However, Mary has a mediating role to strengthen prayer. So, in all cases, one prays to God, because otherwise it is not a prayer anyway. And Jesus himself adds a little extra:

> For where two or three are gathered in my name, I am there among them.
> Matthew 18:20

Praying and helping

Praying has a strong link with helping and being helped. We hear Jesus say at the end of his life:

> And I will ask the Father, and he will give you another Advocate, to be with you forever. John 14:16

Helpfulness is a divine virtue that we may appropriate in order to grow into a full-fledged human being. The monks in the monasteries, who get up very early, just to pray, do not start their prayer with the words of Psalm 40:13 for nothing.

> Be pleased, O Lord, to deliver me;
> O Lord, make haste to help me.

This is how the Church interprets this line. We can pray directly to God in our need, but it is also possible to pray, thanks to the mediation of Mary, or of someone else in your environment or church.

"Behold, your mother!" says Jesus to the entire Church, for us, we who are the Church. The prayer through the intercession of Mary or the other saints or angels is a so-called prayer of intercession. Literally, this is the prayer of coming between, that is, for reconciliation. Asking someone to pray for us is the highest form of a request for help. The petitioner, so to speak, appeals when all ordinary means have already been tried and proved insufficient. This form of prayer supports our own direct personal prayer to God.

Conversely, an intercession is also our prayer for people who can benefit from our prayer, such as, the sick and victims of violence, but we also pray for a good atmosphere at home, for children and grandchildren, or for people in faraway countries, complete strangers, who have only been presented to us by the news.

You may already sense that there is much more to say about this subject. In this context, it is appropriate to explain only the simple form of address 'Woman' for Mary, as Jesus addresses Mary in the Gospel of John:

> And Jesus said to her, "Woman, what concern is that to you and to me? My hour has not yet come." John 2:4

Our Lady

Especially in the past, people spoke of Jesus with a certain familiar inwardness as Our Lord (In the Netherlands even 'Our Dear Lord'), out of reverence and awe, but also with a sense of committed love. In the same way, Mary was and is addressed with the same tenderness as Our Lady. The address 'Woman' for Mary is hers at the suggestion of the Lord himself. The Church agrees with this, because she sees in Mary the new Eve, who is freed from sin. It goes without saying, according to popular devotion all over the world, that many have adopted and experienced affection for Mary. The Marian title Our Lady is paired with an endlessly long set of particulars:

of Lourdes (France),
of Fatima (Portugal),
of Knock (Ireland),
of Kevelaer (Germany),
of Beauraing (Belgium),
of Banneux (Belgium),
of Czestochowa (Poland),
of Medjugorje (Bosnia-Herzegovina)

of Guadalupe (Mexico) and others.

In many Dutch cities or villages, this list is supplemented with places, such as Maastricht, Sittard, Valkenburg, Thorn, Heiloo, Bolsward, and countless other villages.

How did this come about? In fact, there have been an enormous number of apparitions of Mary all over the world, which are still occurring, even though we do not always hear about them. The Church will investigate each apparition intensively before a veneration is officially approved. What ultimately matters is the firm faith of every believer.

Once, during an introductory meeting, I asked one of the new residents, a 102-year-old woman: "How come you kept praying, even though you have experienced so many bad things?" She gave the following beautiful answer:
"Maybe God gave me everything I have experienced so that I could learn something from it. That is how I have always looked at it. You have to want to adapt again and again and you have to ask God for the strength to do so. For example, the rosary is really something to hold on to. My mother taught me to pray it and I have always continued to do so, because my mother also received her share of life, she always said."

It is up to you to put the accent on what you find valuable for your life. It is to be hoped that youth will adopt the faith. Years ago, my daughter Esther once prayed the Our Father and Hail Mary very quickly at the beginning of a meal, because otherwise the food would get cold. I asked afterwards if it could not be a bit slower. "That's how Aunt Jacqueline always prays," she said. Well, I couldn't deny that. At home, prayers were simply said very quickly.

In summary

Let me summarize the above as follows. We sometimes talk about Our Mother Mary, but that never receives the significance of Our Father, who art in Heaven, the prayer that Jesus teaches us to pray. In this way, the Hail Mary can be regarded as an addition to the Our Father. That is why many people pray the two as a fixed pair of prayers before and after eating. That is a powerful and beautiful tradition that is definitely worth preserving.

The Hail Mary

We often pray the prayer to Mary without thinking much about it. That is not so bad in itself, because you can pray this prayer in the car, for example, just as you can safely make a phone call in the car. In any case, you will have to keep your eyes on the road. So turn off the radio for a moment.

If you pray it at home or in another quiet place, learn to pray with all your heart. That is why it is good to examine the Hail Mary under a magnifying glass to see how it is structured.

We borrow half of the Hail Mary from the Gospel of Luke. This is a gospel that goes into detail about the history of the birth of Jesus. The last part of the

Hail Mary is a prayer that was added by the Church in the course of tradition. There is the structure in three parts:

1. The first part of the prayer are the words of the Archangel Gabriel (Luke 1:28), with which the Angel presents himself to Mary:

Hail, full of grace. The Lord is with you.

This can also be translated:

Rejoice, Gracious One, the Lord is with you.

In the Church, we celebrate the feast of the Annunciation to Mary, as it is popularly called. Officially, it is now called the Annunciation of the Lord. We celebrate this feast on 25 March, exactly nine prenatal months before Christmas.

It is the First Joyful Mystery of the rosary.

2. The second part comes from Luke 1:42. These are the words of Mary's cousin Elizabeth, who is expecting her son John (the Baptist). When Mary entered her house she responds with delight:

Blessed are you among women, and blessed is the fruit of your womb.

This event is celebrated in a feast, namely as the Visitation of Mary on 31 May. Mary visits Elisabeth, who, according to the Gospel of Luke, is six months pregnant. This scene has often been depicted by artists. We pray Elizabeth's welcome of Mary as the Second Joyful Mystery of the rosary.

3. The third part is an addition on the part of the Church. The Council of Ephesus (431) chose the title Mother of God as the most important title for Mary, to indicate the divinity of Jesus. In a sense, the title is confusing because it could be inferred

that Mary is not only the mother of Jesus, as the Son of God, but also of God as such. This council did not want to claim that either. In the Litany of Mary she is therefore wrongly called Mother of the Creator. That comes from an exaggerated popular devotion, which logically cannot be correct, and this saying is of course unbiblical. But then again, popular devotions have strong roots, and that is a good thing, because otherwise they might not even exist.

Around the 16th century, this last part was added to the prayer:

Holy Mary, Mother of God, pray for us sinners now and at the hour of our death. Amen

Precisely because of the mention of the hour of death, it is useful to continue to pray this prayer with the dying, especially since people, in the last moments of life, are familiar with this prayer and encouraged by it. Family members who are no longer so religious can also pray it along. The prayer can support them in those hours of saying goodbye.
Eastern Churches
In the Byzantine Churches, there is a similar variation of the Hail Mary, which reads as follows:

Theotokos and Virgin, Hail Mary, full of grace, the Lord is with you.
Blessed are you among women and blessed is the fruit of your womb, for you have borne the Savior of our souls.

Theotokos means "she who gave birth to God."

The Eastern Orthodox Churches know the so-called *hesychastic prayer* or the prayer of the heart. By repeating this prayer, over and over again, as is done in the West with the rosary, a deeper peace comes into the heart beyond rational thought.

Pentecost: Baptized in Fire

Pentecost is a high feast in Church terms, but whether it gives us a festive feeling now is another question. Well, no. Not like Christmas by contrast. The joy lies more in the experience of an extra day off to enjoy the weather. The feast is somewhat vague for many believers. But still, let us dig into the deeper Christian meaning of Pentecost.

To do this, we have to leaf all the way back to the (second) creation story in the Bible, the story of Adam and Eve. The mistake that people usually make when reading this story is to read it as a beautiful story from times long past. However, this story is intended for all times. That is why the story is full of symbolic imagery, because the mystery of the human can be expressed better in images than in words. The story is certainly not historical; it has a timeless character, as if it were written today, so to speak. In the story, we read that well-known sentence about the origin of man:

> Then the Lord God formed man from the dust of the ground, and breathed into his nostrils the breath of life; and the man became a living being. Genesis 2:7

So, the human was made from earth and then breathed into life. God acts in the creation story, similar to a potter and glassblower, who make their products and artisanal handicrafts.

Earth

In Hebrew, the word for human is *adam*, which comes from a stem meaning to be *red*, and to *sparkle reddishly*. Reverend Pieter Oussoren, who has translated the entire Bible, brings back the colour red in his translation of the verse just mentioned. Then, you can hear how it can sound differently:

> Then the One, God, forms the red-blooded man from dust from the blood-red ground and breathes into his nostrils the breath of life; thus the red-blooded man becomes alive in body and soul.[6]

The true nature of man

The word for earth, land, ground, in Hebrew is *adamah*. A beautiful word relationship with Adam, we may conclude! That says something: so earthly, of the earth, from the earth, that is man. The human being is literally, you could almost say, in another sense, an *earth* being, but then we would rather say

---
6 Naardense Bible, 2004. Translated by Guram Kochi MSc

someone is *grounded*, as rooted in the earth, or he is earthly compared to heavenly. And what is the *nature* of the human being then? Is that only to be of dust?

You are dust, and to dust you shall return (Genesis 3:19b); so we hear on Ash Wednesday when receiving the Ash Cross. Or does the human at the same time come from God, because didn't we just read, that it was God who sculpted man? And which is more important, the clay from which we are sculpted or the One Who, according to a certain idea, sculpted and kneaded us into who we have become? Both are of great importance, because that is how the human beings became human.

This immediately brings to mind what the first creation story in Genesis 1, the story of the seven days of creation, says about the origin of man. It says that God created the human being "according to Our image and likeness." Whatever the case may be, in the creation of man, the Creator took Himself as an example. We humans, male and female, can perhaps be characterized as the God's Self-portrait. It is clear that the nature of the human is originally both earthly and heavenly. The artist and work of art resemble each other.

When Michelangelo carved his enormous statue of Moses, entirely from one block of marble, he struck it with his hammer and shouted: "Speak!!" That is how lifelike his Moses had become. Michelangelo had almost called the great Moses to life from the marble. The artist himself had become like Moses. He had brought the image to life, in its dual meaning, as a statue and as a metaphor.

This bridges the gap to Pentecost, because, on the one hand, the human being is material, but there is also a living fire, in both males and females, a spark of inner fire that transcends the material.

Ashes and the hidden fire

The feast of Pentecost actually begins on Ash Wednesday, a good 100 days before Pentecost. In some churches, the palm branches from the previous year, which the churchgoers brought with them, are burned during the Ash Wednesday celebration. The burnt remains of the branches are crushed a bit, but the ashes are still warm from the fire. That is very appropriate; to give the faithful an ash cross, on that long road to Pentecost, in which the spark of the Easter and Pentecost fires is present. The ashes are still warm, sometimes even hot. The ashes are the symbol of matter, the clay, from which we originated. We humans are of the dust of the earth, earthy and grounded, but at the same time we are ardent, at least, longing for the Divine. God places that longing in us when He gives us the breath of life by blowing air into our nostrils, just as the Risen Jesus breathes new spiritual life into His disciples. This is what the Pentecost version of the evangelist John says:

> When it was evening on that day, the first day of the week, and the doors of the house where the disciples had met were locked for fear of the Jews, Jesus came and stood among them and said, 'Peace be with you.'
> 20 After he said this, he showed them his hands and his side. Then the disciples rejoiced when they saw the Lord.
> 21 Jesus said to them again, "Peace be with you. As the Father has sent me, so I send you."
> 22 When he had said this, he breathed on them and said to them, "Receive the Holy Spirit.

23 If you forgive the sins of any, they are forgiven them; if you retain the sins of any, they are retained." John 20:19-23

Completion through forgiveness

In this Easter and Pentecost story by John, the Creator from the book of Genesis is at work, who once, in the beginning, breathed the breath of life into the nostrils of his newly formed human being (Genesis 2:7). It is history that not only repeats itself, but also reaches its completion.

And yet this fulfillment has not yet been fully accomplished. Jesus sends His disciples into the world, just as He himself was sent by the Father. Their learning and apprenticeship period is over. They have now been baptized in the Holy Spirit and are able to fly out of the nest like young birds. When the Risen One appears to them, the disciples know that the end of Jesus' earthly mission has come. Jesus prepared His disciples well and told them that they would continue to experience the love of the Father.

Jesus is also speaking about you, about us, in this time. If we continue to love the Father, He will reveal Himself to us. We receive inner knowledge of the triune God! People who pray every day, even just before going to sleep, experience this inner awareness. Many people find this practice quite normal. "I learned this from my parents," they say. But do you know that you maintain a warm bond with God in this way, do you know how special that is?! Do you know that your daily prayer is a royal distinction in the Kingdom of God?

Just as there are elderly people who have daily contact with their children or with family or friends, so it is, in your daily prayer, that the heavenly Father visits you! You do not see your relatives all day long, but you know that they are there. Knowing this gives you courage and joy. It is exactly the same with your faith. You know that God is there for you. Being loved by God and loving Him give the peace that Jesus speaks about. Earlier, just before His death, He said to His disciples:

> 24 Whoever does not love me does not keep my words; and the word that you hear is not mine, but is from the Father who sent me.
> 25 I have said these things to you while I am still with you.
> 26 But the Advocate, the Holy Spirit, whom the Father will send in my name, will teach you everything, and remind you of all that I have said to you.
> 27 Peace I leave with you; my peace I give to you. I do not give to you as the world gives. Do not let your hearts be troubled, and do not let them be afraid. John 14:24-27

Jesus gives us a deep peace, deep in our hearts, a peace that no person can give us, nor take away, because it is a divine peace. With and in that peace, He sends His disciples into the world as a fire that can multiply rapidly. However, where walls of irreconcilability stand, without breaking down by the power of forgiveness, the disciples of Jesus still have much work to do. Where sins have not (yet) been forgiven, where people continue to stand against each other, with hard heads, the atmosphere of war will continue. And only when such an atmosphere of war is transformed into an atmosphere of forgiveness and justice shall, as the Apostle Paul says, *And the peace of God, which surpasses all understanding, will guard your hearts and your minds in Christ Jesus (Philippians*

4:7). Then the feast of Pentecost reaches its true climax and there is joy in everyone's heart.

And what about the fire?

But where has the well-known fire of Pentecost gone in this story of John, you wonder? Fire is an element from the beginning of the Acts of the Apostles. There, Jesus' disciples are gathered with Mary, the Church is in its birth stage, after the Ascension of the Lord, and they receive the fire of the Holy Spirit, the breath of God, as it is sometimes said.

Now that they have become fiery people, they immediately proclaim the Word in all languages and dialects; there is no more Babel or confusion of tongues: *Each one heard them speaking in the native language of each* the story says (Acts 2:5). The one language of faith is then understood by everyone. Here the fullness of the fulfillment of salvation comes into view, which is so characteristic of the feast of Pentecost, 50 days after Easter. God and the human and the people among themselves understand each other again. They feel each other deeply. There is no more miscommunication.

Fire as a symbol of the Divine

Where fire is presented so emphatically, it must come from God, biblically speaking. The churchgoing believer has noticed the fire before Pentecost, namely during Easter night when the first fire arose from flint. Actually, it should be that flint has been struck and ignited to make a spark, the early beginning of the new Easter fire. Then the fire maker, as generations before us did, must carefully blow the flame into a larger flame, of course without blowing out the fire. After all, new life is vulnerable; it cannot yet withstand storms and yet it is soon as strong as a small beech tree, that is very firmly rooted in the ground. Once the fire is big enough, it will no longer be blown out by the storm but it will instead be fanned.

The Pentecost story from Acts begins with the Creator blowing fire, which was felt like the wind of a rising storm. Just as fire on Easter night, now on Pentecost, the divine spark in man, in his soul, is blown into a flame:

> When the day of Pentecost had come, they were all together in one place.
> 2 And suddenly from heaven there came a sound like the rush of a violent wind, and it filled the entire house where they were sitting.
> 3 Divided tongues, as of fire, appeared among them, and a tongue rested on each of them.
> 4 All of them were filled with the Holy Spirit and began to speak in other languages, as the Spirit gave them ability. Acts 2:1-4

Balance between being grounded and ardor

The flame of the Paschal candle on Easter night becomes a blazing fire on Pentecost. The person who perceives fire within him will do well to preserve and guard it in a balanced way. Being grounded, and, at the same time, in ardor, earthly and heavenly; to balance each other out. The person who is too earthly lives too materially, too much from his passions, too focused on possessions and personal gain. Remarkably enough, we also see this extremity in steadfast believers, who sometimes cling too rigidly to rituals as if no deeper growth of faith is possible.

On the one hand, the human being can be compared to the rich young man who wants to follow Jesus but who is afraid of becoming perfect. Afraid to let go of his possessions, his titles, his status, and everything he has acquired (see Matthew 19:16-22). On the other hand, people are sometimes too fervent when they are inclined to make overconfident resolutions, at the risk of losing contact with everyday reality. This was evident in the attitude of the apostle Peter, who wanted to follow Jesus wherever He would go, but who realized too late that he had already denied the Lord, as Jesus had predicted. Therefore, the risen Lord asked him three times later whether he really loved Him before He definitely appointed Peter as leader of His Church.

If these two types, the rich young ruler and Peter, do not want to change, they are not resilient enough to endure setbacks. The rich youth went home, disappointed, despite all his initial enthusiasm. Peter in turn "wept bitterly" over his betrayal of Jesus. People who persist in a rigid attitude lose their trust in God more and more, even though they may believe that God sees their pettiness and wants to help them. We hear nothing more about the rich youth in the Gospel, but Peter is steadfast. He retains his characteristic fervor, but knows how to ground his faith in Christ more deeply. This becomes clear when, after the miracle of the tongues of fire, Peter addresses the crowd and testifies, with a fiery speech, that Jesus, once crucified, has now risen. The people may feel guilty over the crucifixion, but Peter, who knows the feeling of guilt, raises the people up and gives them a new perspective:

> Peter said to them, "Repent, and be baptized every one of you in the name of Jesus Christ so that your sins may be forgiven; and you will receive the gift of the Holy Spirit."
> Acts 2:38

A positive turn

The person who is able to give a positive turn to life, again, after a great disappointment, is grounded; he keeps his feet on the ground, while being fiery, enthusiastically daring to take on new challenges. This person will reflect and pray, in the face of setbacks and suffering, and in that process find a new spirituality. The other two, the too earthly and the too fiery person, will also pray, but their prayer will yield less fruit because of insufficient trust in God's redeeming Presence, unless they take new steps. So Jesus says, *Enter through the narrow gate* (Matt 7:13a).

Enhancing spiritual strength

The dividing line between earthly and heavenly is, of course, not black and white. In each of us, the line alters from day to day. We are all a bit of one thing and another. Yet the art of life is to enhance our spiritual strength as we grow older. We certainly need strength more than ever when our physical limitations increase. Then we confront our spiritual disposition, really.

Can we still find joy, even in the fact that we are physically not as strong, and we are more dependent as we get older? With humor, by appreciating what is still possible, by praying, by continuing to move and maintain contacts where possible, we keep ourselves going.

People often struggle, as they grow older, with the question whether they have made the right choices in their lives. This can result in a gnawing feeling. How can we look at the evil in our lives from the vantage point of the end and completion of life, which we celebrate at Pentecost? Not an easy question!

Knowledge of Evil

The second creation story, where the newly created human being is given the breath of life, says that man, nevertheless, against God's will, has acquired the knowledge of evil; it's knowledge that cannot be endure (how topical!). This knowledge transcends his limited cognitive ability. God knew this and that is why He impressed it upon the human being not to pick the fruits of the Tree of Knowledge of Good and Evil. Note that this is not a historical story, it is mythical and imagistic, and it has meaning for us in our time. At the beginning, the human being is still in a state of eternal life. After all, he is with God in Paradise, the actual environment of man. To know evil outside of God, in combination with eternal existence, would lead to a kind of dual godhood. That would be detrimental to the Creator's plan, which God cannot allow:

> 22 Then the Lord God said, "See, the man has become like one of us, knowing good and evil; and now, he might reach out his

> hand and take also from the tree of life, and eat, and live forever" —
> 23 therefore the Lord God sent him forth from the garden of Eden, to till the ground from which he was taken.
> 24 He drove out the man; and at the east of the garden of Eden he placed the cherubim, and a sword flaming and turning to guard the way to the tree of life.
> Genesis 3:22-24

So, looking back on one's own life, one may realize that one should have handled things differently, sometimes. This is in itself a very important fact and gives rise to remorse. One gains perspective to look differently at oneself and one's fellow human beings.

The human being outside Paradise

Back to the Bible story: God is forced to expel the human being from Paradise, but God continues to care for the man and woman until the very end, which shows how much the expulsion grieves God. He remains a caring God: *And the Lord God made garments of skins for the man[a] and for his wife, and clothed them. (Genesis 3:21).*

There is a certain parallel with growing children: at a certain point they must fly and leave the nest of their familiar home. Left to himself, humans must try to survive while being exposed to evil, sin, and death. In principle it's dead end, and though it does not correspond to God's original plan, now God wants this state of separation. There is no alternative. The virus of evil within humans is to be destroyed with death, but God desires to preserve human beings, in any case, and to give us back our paradisiacal state. God upholds His original idea, which hasn't changed. That is the deeper message of the story.

How can this tide be turned? We make a big leap in history. There seems to be only one definite way out: the Creator becomes a creature! However bizarre, it happens with the birth of Jesus. We celebrate this at Christmas. In Jesus, as God of course and therefore also as a man, there is no trace of evil, sin, violence, or death to be found, because He is eternally born of God. You know the text about this from our confession of faith. We confess therein:

I believe in one Lord Jesus Christ, the Only Begotten Son of God, born of the Father before all ages. God from God, Light from Light, true God from true God, begotten, not made, consubstantial with the Father; through Him all things were made. For us men and for our salvation He came down from heaven, and by the Holy Spirit was incarnate of the Virgin Mary, and became man.

Jesus as a Trailblazer

With Jesus, there was a human being on earth who lived and achieved eternal life, in accordance with God's original intention. Throughout His life, He remained invulnerable to any aversion to God. For a brief moment, He was truly a heavenly King on earth, when he entered Jerusalem on a donkey to a great welcome. It was unique event in human history. Thanks to Him, we celebrate at Easter that the gate to eternal life is open in principle for everyone who wants to enter.

I personally think that this extends to every person who has lived with good intentions and has committed himself to his fellow man, despite the great mistakes that this person may have made in his life, so long as he has remorse for them. In essence, we are to be (or to have been) a good person. Speaking of good and evil.

He Who came back from the Dead!

The good news of Easter is that Jesus is indeed someone who came back from the dead, although people often claim sarcastically that no one has ever returned from heaven. After Easter, the risen Jesus returns by appearing to His disciples for no less than forty days until he ascends to heaven. On the fortieth day after Easter, we celebrate Ascension Day. The completion of these holy events is realized on Pentecost.

Pentecost and the Fire

Ten days after Ascension Day on Pentecost, the Jewish feast of the renewal of the Covenant, the disciples—that is, standing for us as believers—are baptized in the Holy Spirit. What God did, when He created man, happens again: He breathed "the breath of life" into man. It is then the fiftieth day after Easter with fifty being the number representing the fullness of God's covenant with humanity. The symbol of the fire is central.

The fire burns away the evil in man. The person who is on fire on Pentecost is completely and utterly cleansed by receiving the Holy Spirit. The Spirit is the Breath of God. Man, Adam, receives the breath in a renewal of his soul, and with that, he regains paradise with God.

This is like being overshadowed by the Spirit, which happens to Mary when she miraculously conceives (Luke 1:39). Thus, she was present with the disciples at Pentecost, perhaps we may say as the Mother of the Church, and there she received, once again, with the disciples, the power and fire of the Holy Spirit, through which the community of Jesus' disciples receives the breath as a new life force.

Meaning of all this for us

What does receiving the Holy Spirit, the Breath of God, mean now for and in our daily life of faith? The story of faith seems to be inverted in Pentecost. Where believer is living in God with Baptism, after Pentecost God comes to live in man, as Jesus says:

> Those who love me will keep my word, and my Father will love them, and we will come to them and make our home with them. John 14:23

The believer then becomes the new temple of God's Presence.

The function of the Holy Spirit, as Jesus said, is to remind us of all Jesus' words. That is why the Bible is so important, because it is a prayerful remembrance of God. The Bible is our Helper and Comforter, as Eve was created as a helper for Adam. We pray to the Father with Jesus' words in us.

In summary

At Christmas, Jesus is born as the new human with divine knowledge of good and evil. At Easter, Jesus breaks through as God-human to eternal life, thanks to His non-violent response to anyone who wants to do Him harm. And at Pentecost, the restored and recreated human receives breath by God's Breath. The circle is complete again. People still die, but eternal death is no longer there. Jesus says to the repentant criminal who is also crucified next to Him:

> Truly I tell you, today you will be with me in Paradise. Luke 23:43

So the way is shown to overcome the virus of evil.

Pigeon story 1

Sometimes something new just blows in and in this case comes flying in. The cherry season is announced by the beautiful white spring blossom. In the spring, the blossoms look like one big bridal bouquet. The growing cherries benefit from lots of sunshine.

The cherries become increasingly red. They are a feast for the eyes, but not just for the human eye. The pigeons keep a watchful eye over them, too. Especially those fat pigeons watch their seasonal meal shining from afar. From one day to the next, they completely devour a small cherry tree. You have to be there like a shot, or a cock in the bush, to secure the last harvest for your own household. So get up early in the morning to pick the last cherries barefoot, and still in your dressing gown, before those five gray fatties have their turn grazing.

The fact that birds get their share is not such a disaster in itself. It is the humor of Mother Nature. You now see how eager pigeons can be. They contribute to the spread of cherry pits, and it is to be hoped that many garden owners will appreciate the growing tree at its true value. And may the pigeon manure prove to be of suitable quality (unfortunately, this is usually not the case).

The cherry harvest may only be a modest bowlful this year, but for next year, it is better to make wicked plans in time and set up a garden net.

Pigeon story 2

A completely different story with a pigeon in the leading role was the Pentecost experience of my old father in The Hague. On Pentecost Sunday, of all days, he heard strange noises from the living room, on the upper floor, as if all sorts of things were falling down. He quickly went to investigate, and to his amazement, he saw a pigeon sitting in his study. The bird had probably come in through the balcony door of the bedroom and had calmly walked around the house. This learned dove had made a huge mess of things, in the meantime, and, possibly in a panic, had left some smelly treats behind. I asked if this could be the Holy Spirit of Pentecost, but my father was not exactly convinced. And he was right, because on Pentecost, the Spirit does not appear in the form of a dove but as fire!

We have already seen the descending dove at the Baptism of Jesus in the Jordan. There the dove reminds us of the dove that Noah once released, in the story of the flood, to find out whether land was in sight.

Since a dove on Pentecost cannot be the Holy Spirit, there was sufficient reason to gently coerce this drifting cherry eater into the air.

Your soul

*If your ears no longer hear,
may your soul listen.*

*If your eyes no longer see,
may your soul see.*

*If your nose no longer smells,
may your soul sniff.*

*If your tongue no longer tastes,
may your soul get a taste.*

*If your arms can no longer lift,
may your soul carry you.*

*If your hands no longer caress,
may your soul kiss.*

If your legs no longer carry you,

*may your soul bring you forth.
If your feet no longer walk,
may your soul walk.*

*If your lungs are short of breath,
may your soul breathe life into you.*

*If your whole body starts to hurt,
may your soul ease your pain
and comfort you.*

*And if your mind loses its clarity,
your soul will not forget who you are.*

*And if it is your heart that stops beating,
then your soul
will rejoice and become happy.*

*May your soul on that day
look upon its Healer
and recognize and belong to Him:
He, Who has always been there,
He, Who wants to keep you,*

*May your soul then come Home
into the Father's Heart.*

Finding a foothold in prayer

All kinds of mixed thoughts and feelings arise around prayer. The first thought, and assumption, is that praying should yield something. We have all become results-oriented thinkers. If something does not yield anything, then what good is it? It is like ordering something these days: we expect it to arrive today or tomorrow, at the latest. If not, the service is bad or even the company, and we will never go and order anything from them, again. We have become spoiled these days and impatient too! When we start talking about praying, we may begin with the idea that the results must be delivered today; well, if we make that assumption, then we will be very disappointed. Then, we will get a bad taste in our mouth about the company, God & Co, which in our eyes offers worthless service—much too late.

Could it be that we think like this because we consider in advance: "If God exists, why doesn't he do anything about the misery in the world?" Or we make another assumption: there is misery in the world, and, you see, God doesn't exist anyway, and so praying is pointless. Or we shout: "They lied to us all in the past!"

Prayer imparts to the believer a stable state of mind. This emanates from a trust in God gained from experience. Jesus calls upon His disciples, to ask the Father in His Name for anything they want. This offers us at least an inner satisfaction. Gradually, the person praying learns what it means to pray "in Jesus' Name," namely that we are to pray according to God's will. This in turn means that prayer has everything to do with what God sees as good for us, namely what brings us as human beings closer to God. Praying for a better income can also be good, but a better income does not necessarily bring you closer to God. In praying, one notices over time that prayer offers a permanent point of rest, a real support in difficult times.

In conversation

Praying is communicating with God. This can be compared to our contact with people. In our daily interactions, talking with another means a mutual conversation. Do you ever doubt whether the person to whom you are speaking really exists? On the phone, it can get quiet on the other end. "Are you still there?," we ask. "Yes, I'm listening," replies the person on the other side. Then the conversation continues until we end it after a few minutes or a few hours. (My wife sometimes spends two hours on the phone with her sister, who lives a street and a half away!) Such conversations are a relief, they give peace or information, they helps one to move on. Did we have a good conversation or did we just wish to hear each other's voice? That is also important if you don't have the chance to see each other in person. During the corona virus period, we occasionally zoomed, which is video calling, but that wasn't quite like being together, to be honest.

In prayer

Be that as it may, prayer can be well compared to conversation. But what exactly is prayer? Above, we talked about praying for results, but the Jewish scholar Abraham Joshua Heschel rightly remarks on this in a very heartfelt way:

Indeed, to pray does not only mean to seek help; it also means to seek Him.[7]

Many people say that if they could, they would pray, but they think they can't. My father once responded, in this context: "If you want to, you can!" That is true in a sense, but there's a lot that we want to do that we can't do. For example, there was a very beautiful girl in my class at school. If I looked at her from the side, my cheeks would turn red and warm. When she turned toward me, I would of course quickly duck. To look at her was quite a task, let

---

7 Abraham Joshua Heschel, God in Search of Man: a Philosophy of Judaism, p.28. First HARPER TORCHBOOK edition published 1966 by Harper & Row, Publishers, Incorporated, 49 East 33rd Street New York, N.Y. 10016.

alone speak to her. What on earth could I say without sounding terribly stupid?

When I met my wife, I was fortunately a bit farther along in the art of seduction, and I said, in no time at all, like a shot with the bow: I love you!! Well, her whole family heard about that, for years afterward, and they always laughed heartily. What matters is that my declaration worked to break the ice, and she was moved to say at least something very sweet back. The fact that everyone laughed about this anecdote afterwards only fills me with pride. At least I got my loot! To anyone who wants to try praying, speak to your Father in heaven for you may see and call Him by that name:

DEAR FATHER, I LOVE YOU!

Just try it, just like that, without really knowing what you are saying. Because remember: even the most skilled person praying knows just as little about their words. To pray without mystery, without rising above yourself, remains all too human. And because saying "I love you" once is not enough, you keep repeating it all day long, as the Apostle Paul says:

> Pray without ceasing. 1 Thess 5:17

Praying and loving

Praying expresses therefore an infinite love, but you cannot say of loving: "Only when I have time, or feel like it, or I am not too tired, or as long as it does not cost any money." Of course, that is not how love works.

A good start is half the battle. It also means persevering and not giving up if you feel that your prayer is not answered immediately.

Breathing

But pray without ceasing? How on earth are we supposed to imagine that? Christians in Orthodox Churches (in Russia, Greece, Bulgaria, Romania, and the Ukraine) put it this way. Every person has breath. Hopefully, breathing continues incessantly, just like your heartbeat. If your heart stops, you are dead, and if your breathing stops, ditto. Orthodox Christian people of prayer therefore teach one to pray the prayer of the heart, in rhythm with the breath and the heartbeat, in short, the Jesus Prayer:

Lord Jesus Christ, Son of God (when breathing in)
Have mercy on me, a sinner (when breathing out)

This prayer is taken from the words of blind Bartimaeus, who was begging along the road between Jerusalem and Jericho. When he heard that Jesus was coming, he started to shout very loudly:

> Jesus, Son of David, have mercy on me!

He shows us who we are. We too are sitting along the road of life and we beg for God's mercy. We too are, as it were, blind and we do not see Jesus. We hope that He will come by one day and He will call us and also ask us, just as He asked blind Bartimaeus:

> ""What do you want me to do for you?"

And hopefully we too will say just in time:

> "My teacher, let me see again."
> Mark 10-47: 51

May it indeed be so that we may now, at least, see what is important in our lives. And keep hoping that we will ultimately see Him Who is our destination. So listen carefully when He comes by! Prick up your ears!!

Praying with a prayer rope

To aid their Jesus prayer, to be prayed incessantly, Eastern Christians have a cloth prayer rope that is comparable to our rosary.

For example, accompanied by this prayer string, one may repeat the Jesus Prayer continuously. Anyone who applies themselves with some determination will get used to the prayer after a relatively short time. The prayer, indeed, merges in rhythm with your breathing and your heartbeat. After a few weeks, the prayer, so to speak, will start to pray itself. A strange idea, but true! For example, while walking or upon waking up, and even in your sleep and dreams, the prayer may begin to pray itself without your explicit decision, "I'm going to pray." The prayer becomes like that nice (or annoying) melody that keeps ringing in your mind.

The Spirit prays in us

The Spirit of God who prays in you, the Spirit as the Breath of God, lifts you toward the transcendent, as you reach out to God by this prayer. The Jesus Prayer is therefore a prayer that everyone can pray, young or old, learned or not, sick or healthy; everyone lives from the Jesus Prayer in the Christian East. People who often pray the rosary will imagine very well what this practice is about. By the way, you can pray the Jesus Prayer on your rosary, and your ten fingers; it makes no difference to your breathing!
Anyone who prays the Jesus Prayer and/or the rosary will soon notice that body and mind come into harmony. They will settle into a feeling of peace and tranquility.

Praying and Fasting in Secret

Incidentally, regarding the cooperation of body and mind, Jesus explains fasting: both praying and fasting come into their own in secret, a silent space of the heart, to strengthen the awareness that this is done together with God. Praying and fasting join forces to focus the whole person even more strongly on Him. Jesus thinks from the inside out, from the heart, where God sees in secret. In the Sermon on the Mount, Jesus speaks about this principle (Matthew 6).

In order to be aware, and to experience distinctly what's hidden, Jesus urges you to take a seat in your inner room (or closet). The inner room at that time was the storage room, similar in Europe to the cupboard or cellar at the stairs. "No one sees you there, but only your heavenly Father," says Jesus. You do not have to pretend to be more beautiful than you are. You are already beautiful enough for God.

Both praying and fasting are difficult for the believer, at first, and take a lot of getting used to, but perseverance pays off! Most important is it to believe that it is God himself Who prays in you! Praying is never an achievement of our own, it is the work of God in us. The goal is for humans to become one with God and then one with their fellows.

Every prayer from the heart is good

The Jewish tradition has beautiful stories about prayer: how you should and should not pray. Their learning, great knowledge, and warm experience of the biblical texts, and their constant passing on of them to the next generations—for the Jews, this has all together produced an impressive treasure trove. Nevertheless, they are very well aware of the danger of vanity and self-righteousness in prayer. In order to lead us back onto a healthy track, moral anecdotes are told. Here is a Jewish story, which I once heard, but unfortunately I no longer remember its origins.

In a working-class neighborhood, a poor worker was praying by the open window. Actually, he no longer knew how to pray officially, so he prayed in his own words: "Lord, help me. Lord, help me."

At that moment, a law scholar was walking through the street and heard the worker praying. He stopped, listened for a while, and then thought that he could give the worker a few tips on how to pray better. Then his prayer would surely be answered sooner.

He called the man and said that God likes to hear people praise and thank Him for all His blessings. He taught the man a beautiful traditional prayer. The man thanked the scholar heartily, but the latter had long since moved on.

The good man went to pray like that, but the next day he did not know exactly how it went. "My way of praying was apparently not good enough, so I will never pray again," the worker thought to himself.

In heaven, however, the Eternal-Praised-Be-He suddenly missed one of His most precious prayers. That night He appeared to the law scholar in a dream and urged him to jump out of bed and rush like a hare to the poor worker to tell him that he absolutely must not give up the prayer he had always been used to praying.

Deeply impressed, the law scholar returned again. And the worker...he became the most blessed in the whole city!

This story teaches us not to be arrogant. Faithful believers, and sincere people of prayer, should not scorn those who say they do not believe in God or the commandments. They shouldn't be regarded as less than they are. It could well be that the one single prayer that a so-called unbeliever prays in his need, or before going to sleep, will find a greater audience with God than a prayer by someone that goes exactly by the book.

The moral of the story is that prayer is effective when it is praying from the heart as Jesus says.

But whenever you pray, go into your room and shut the door and pray to your Father who is in secret; and your Father who sees in secret will reward you. Matthew 6:6

Hold onto life through prayer

In this way, your hold on life is established through prayer on a solid foundation. This is within the possibilities of every person, despite the thresholds that the novice prayer may need to overcome. Let the Spirit of God do it in you, and then everything will be fine!

Remembering and commemorating

Normally, in the autumn, the day after the feast of All Saints, we commemorate our dear deceased in church. This good custom is increasingly being honored outside the Church. Apparently, this annual commemoration meets a deep need.

Strictly speaking, it is impossible to really say goodbye. Perhaps that is because our deceased have helped shape us as the people we have become. You do not meet people in your life for no reason. It therefore goes against our instincts that they should be taken out of our lives. All the more so, because they have been of great significance to us and actually still are.

Timelessness

Be that as it may, death remains a natural fact that is inherent to our temporary existence. At the same time, the human spirit knows how to rise above the temporary. Our spirit experiences infinity. For example, some forms of art or music have a timeless dimension. In that atmosphere, we experience an awareness of our loved ones. They are not bus passengers who sit with us on a bus as passers-by. Our loved ones are not outside of us, but inside of us, in our hearts. They live in us and we in them, that is, within that infinite space of our spiritual heart.

Hard blow

When a loved one dies, many elderly people experience a blow, similar to the experience of being alone after years of a good marriage. They suddenly find themselves in a situation in which they are separated from one other unintentionally. They have never thought about separation – about that very idea – and then, suddenly, their health breaks down and their familiar life is over. That is a hard blow in all cases. There is nothing left but to put the shards together again, somehow.

The temporality of existence seems to be victorious, at such a moment, over the desire of love that transcends time. It is precisely at those moments that remembrance comes alive powerfully. Whether religious or not, people do their best to keep alive what has been there. Everyone does that. Every year we commemorate events with a strong personal meaning. When someone dies, the thought of him or her should not die, because if it did, then their death will be real, it is said.

Truly, the living spirit fights against the body that is doomed to die! Remembrance is an attempt to overcome the temporality of the physical.

Re-experienced inwardly

Remembrance is more than a ritual, it is spiritual. This aspect is expressed in the word remembering itself: to re-experience the thought inwardly. And in the same way, re-thinking is a new consideration of our previous experiences (including thoughts and feelings). In this way, what seemed to be the past becomes present again. This remembering has a spiritual value: it strengthens the spirit and keeps it alive in difficult times and then directs the gaze to the future.

It is said: "Life goes on." If we do not take responsibility for life ourselves, others will do it for us. Remembering and commemorating make it possible to bring everything that has passed into the now of today. This is thanks to the timeless and infinite dimension of our human spirit. The past can become the present and the present can become the future. Our spirit continues to search for deeper answers and meanings. And the spirit itself: it does adapt. It is flexible enough. In this way, what has seemed impossible becomes possible, after all.

Searching for God

For the believer, the spiritual search is the search for God, the Eternal. The search for the Higher involves a movement forward, a next road to embark on, until the final destination is reached. People who do not believe probably no longer see a final destination. Of course, they are no less human for that. On the contrary, every person is unique. The Jewish scholar Abraham Joshua Heschel said, regarding people and faith, that human beings only come into their own when the person is convinced that God is looking for him. So, it could be the other way around, too.

Faith, remembering and commemorating, therefore, have everything to do with an open and receptive attitude, which, in turn, presupposes an active search by us. Being human alternates between searching and being found. Abraham Joshua Heschel puts it this way:

Two sources of religious thinking are given us: memory (tradition) and personal insight. We must rely on our memory and we must strive for fresh insight. We hear from tradition, we also understand through our own seeking.

Heschel continues:

"If a man says to you, I have labored and not found, do not believe him. If he says, I have not labored but still have found, do not believe him. If he says, I have labored and found, you may believe him." It is true that in seeking Him we are assisted by Him[8].

---

8 Abraham Joshua Heschel, God Seeks Man: a Philosophy of Judaism, p.27-28. First HARPER TORCHBOOK edition published 1966 by Harper & Row, Publishers, Incorporated, 49 East 33rd Street New York, N.Y. 10016.

Sacred by nature

Now, with all the attention on the climate and the better treatment of the earth, I keep missing references and honor to the people who used to live in complete balance with nature for centuries: the indigenous peoples, who now seem to be westernizing, to some extent.

We, too, still recall our mothers sitting behind their sewing machines or knitting and darning socks by the fireplace. The lives of people back then were, indeed, hard, but there was more cohesion and unity at that time—unity, especially, with the community to which they were a part.

Other cultures

The world and the culture of the indigenous human beings were of a piece with the natural environment. They lived in harmony with plants and wild animals. They only hunted to have necessary food, never too much, because excess could be harmful for the future. And all this came from their realization that their entire living environment was and is a great spiritual unity. There was no gap between young people and old people, as there is in modern society, today. The elderly were eager to pass on their traditions and the young were curious about the secrets of life.

In Zimbabwe, for example, old age is essential. While in other cultures people make an impression by boasting about how young they seem or want to continue to feel, in Africa people want people to know how old they are. Because there, old age is a blessing and not a curse. The older you get, the more you are respected. Old age has to do with wisdom and a certain familiarity with the world of your ancestors, with whom you've maintained a bond beyond death.

One with heaven

So people were also in unity with heaven. They knew, from early morning to late evening—and of course at night—that they were dependent on the elements. This unity made people humble, in an appropriate way.

Those who bring heaven and earth into balance, within themselves, experience a unified whole.

That means holiness. Regardless of whether we believe or not, every person has within a holy desire for unity.

Our shortcomings break that sense of unity, sadly. When asked, "How are you?", many older people reply, "It just has to be." We have to piece our lives together from all sorts of fragments. Help for each other in this process provides comfort and restores a measure of our original coherence. To support one another, in the brokenness of life, is very important and very well possible.

To grow closer to one another by curiosity without splitting hairs is healing, curative, and therefore, a holy pursuit. To contribute to a good and pleasant atmosphere among ourselves is even health-promoting. We sleep better if we can start the night with a peaceful heart.

Those who sleep well are, of course, less tired and less irritated during the day. Perhaps it is a surprising thought that having an eye for a harmonious atmosphere in the home may have something to do with holiness!

All saints

Fortunately, the original unity of heaven and earth, and our connection with nature, is preserved somewhat by the holy rhythm of our own church liturgy, which follows the rhythms of nature. Those sensitive to nature and the liturgy, both, will experience this cohesion easily. Each season has its own atmosphere and intimacy. You can think of the following. Take for example the light of the longest day, which is often very soft and mysterious in the late evening. The sun illuminates the clouds between 22:00

and 22:30, which reflect that nighttime light back to the earth.

Birth celebrations of John the Baptist and Jesus in connection with nature

About the longest day, on June 24, the birth of John the Baptist is celebrated. Yes, this is exactly 6 months before Jesus was born, in the dark Christmas night, during the about shortest day of the year.

In earlier times, people, or rather the Church, have linked the secrets of faith to natural phenomena. And that was not such a strange idea at all, because nature and faith have in common that they transcend the human. So, there gradually emerged in Church tradition an exuberant celebration of the holidays. The logic of nature, therefore, and all kinds of old traditions have been examined very carefully, especially those traditions that we encounter in the Bible. This idea is confirmed in many old weather proverbs, which served as a guideline for farmers.

Thus, the birth of John the Baptist, as the forerunner of Jesus, is linked to the beginning of summer and that of Jesus to the beginning of winter: the light of the sun diminishes day by day after John's birth because the days become shorter. But after Jesus' birth, the sun becomes increasingly stronger and more prolonged. After all, the days become longer, because Jesus is the Light, the Sun that rises in our hearts! The transition from the shortest to the longest day therefore invigorates our sense of faith. Jesus, John the Baptist, Mary, and Joseph are the most striking holy persons from the beginning of church history. With them, we come close to the basic biblical idea: "Only God is holy" (Rev 4:8). Have you ever thought about what holy actually means? It comes from heil or whole. Whoever is happy feels whole, healed. Completely complete, nothing is missing from your happiness, both physically and mentally: it's a Holy Day!, holiday, because in the past people had the day off on days of the saints.

All Saints Day (1 November) and All Souls Day (2 November)

In the early days of Christianity, the baptized were automatically called saints. In fact, these were all ordinary believers.

When people in those early Christian times were confronted with terrible persecutions, people were forced to make choices. You were for the Emperor or for Jesus. People who refused to make sacrifices to the Emperor of Rome were often horribly tortured and they died. They themselves only became happier because they were uniting more closely with Christ. And so, the day of a martyr's death turned into the day of a new spiritual birth.

With their heroic deaths, the martyrs were great examples for all believers. There were moments, more and more, when martyrs were commemorated. People started to visit the churches where they were buried. The number of saints increased to such an extent that, around the year 1000, Rome introduced November 1 as a gathering day for all the saints, the high feast of All Saints Day. In Belgium and Germany this feast is still a holiday. This festival has been linked to the Celtic commemoration of the deceased: All Souls Day. That was a logical idea, because the heavenly and earthly community of saints is, of course, a single united whole.

In the Protestant churches, the veneration of saints has always remained controversial. Catholic and Eastern Christians nevertheless draw much inspiration and support for their faith from the lives of saints. For example, in the old "Catholiek Housebook" (p.93) by Benedictine Father Dom. A. Beekman says:

It goes without saying that the veneration of saints should not overwhelm the celebration of the Mysteries of Redemption, because these are the great feasts of the Church Year, the main moments that should shine in full splendor, because they are of the utmost importance for our soul life. The saints are still our intercessors in Heaven with God, to whom we will never appeal in vain.[9]

---

9 Dom. A. Beekman OSB, Katholiek Huisboek – Liturgische gedachten, gebruiken, lezingen, gebeden en wenken voor het katholieke gezin N.V.Uitgevers Mij.Diligentia, Amsterdam, p.93. Translated by Guram Kochi MSc

Redemption

Some beautiful old words are unfortunately in danger of disappearing from our language. Redemption is such a word. This word has a connection with the unloading of a ship, which is relieved of its cargo. (Redemption is verlossing in Dutch, while lossen means "unloading" in Dutch.)

In the same way, we as humans also have a cargo, from which would rather be free. It is the burden of the negative, evil, dissatisfaction, discontent, which burdens the human being. To burden: : sometimes we experience others as heavy and also ourselves. We carry with us the heavy burden of all the setbacks we've experienced in the past. In traditional church lore, our life already began with this burden: we were born with primordial sin.

People can grumble endlessly about all sorts of things, especially the elderly. The mission of Jesus is to redeem us from all that, from all evil tendencies, from our sins, which perhaps we ourselves suffer from the most: "For He shall accomplish the salvation of His people from their sins" (Mt. 1:21). Without that heavy burden, the human becomes light in weight. Jesus is our inner reliever of burdens. The Bible gives Him the title Redeemer. One of His most encouraging sayings is this one.

> Come to me, all you that are weary and are carrying heavy burdens, and I will give you rest.
> 29 Take my yoke upon you, and learn from me; for I am gentle and humble in heart, and you will find rest for your souls.
> 30 For my yoke is easy, and my burden is light. Matt 11:28-30

As long as humans have existed, we have the tendency to deny or minimize the moral evil within ourselves, to trivialize it: "It's not that bad and it can't do any harm and who cares about it?" We have difficulty with the concept of sin. Evil, which is anchored in ourselves, does not go away so easily. Breaking free from evil and being able to let go is the work of a lifetime.

Let us humbly acknowledge that, as people to be redeemed, we nevertheless become people who can live from the inner heart, where God is our source of life. Once this realization is anchored in our thinking, we become joyful, because redemption has to do with finally being set free, so that one can, once again, perceive the original calling to holiness.

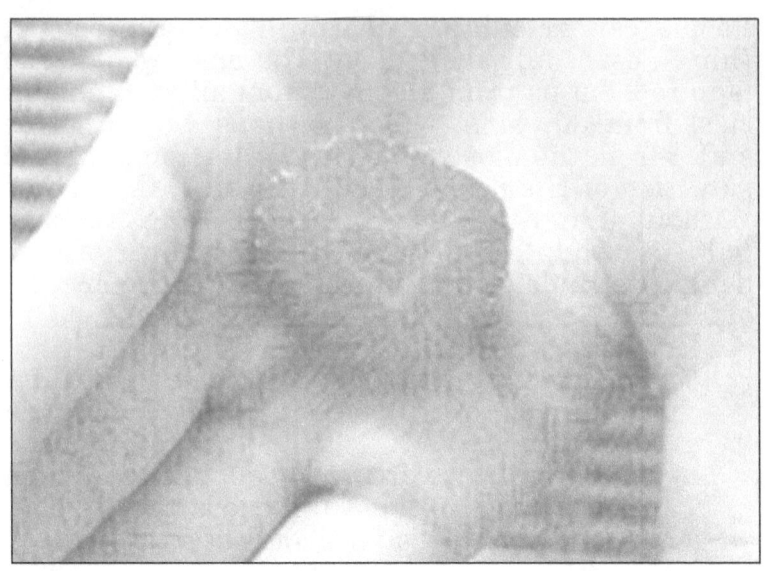

Gifts for the Redeemer. Christmas meditation

Now *a child has been born for us, a son given to us. Isaiah 9:6* Now that this lasting gift from heaven has been destined for us, the question is how we, in turn, are moved and touched by this deep gift given.

The wise men saw a star from afar and the shepherds saw an angel up close. Shepherds and wise men: they kept an eye on heaven.

Speaking of the view of heaven: I was once in the car with my children on the way to the Christmas circus during the Christmas holidays. They had said that I was a bit grumpy. I was indeed tired and moody. Suddenly my son exclaimed, in broad daylight: "Oh, look, the moon!" The half moon was visible against the blue afternoon sky. This was suddenly such a different reality that I completely forgot my bad mood. This is key: to break through what's closed to open to the greatness of God's hidden salvation.

The two Christmas stories

In the middle of a winter night, heaven opened up for us. And what did you see and what was your reaction? You may have seen a beautiful nativity scene somewhere. On display there was a combination of stories. The ox and the donkey are mentioned in the prophecy of Isaiah, the shepherds come from the Gospel of Luke, the wise men (literally magi or magicians) appear in the Gospel of Matthew.

A universal human is born

One thing is clear, namely that a human being of universal value/significance was born. How did those directly involved know that? Mary, the mother of the Lord, heard it from the angel:

> And now, you will conceive in your womb and bear a son, and you will name him Jesus. He will be great, and will be called the Son of the Most High, and the Lord God will give to him the throne of his ancestor David. He will reign over the house of Jacob for ever, and of his kingdom there will be no end. Luke 1:31-33

And it is also an angel who reassures Joseph with the words:

> But just when he had resolved to do this, an angel of the Lord appeared to him in a dream and said, "Joseph, son of David, do not be afraid to take Mary as your wife, for the child conceived in her is from the Holy Spirit. 21 She will bear a son, and you are to name him Jesus, for he will save his people from their sins." Matt 1:20-21

The wise men then asked King Herod:

> Where is the child who has been born king of the Jews? For we observed his star at its rising, and have come to pay him homage. Matt 2:2

and the angel said to the shepherds:

> To you is born this day in the city of David a Saviour, who is the Messiah [Christ], the Lord. Luke 2:11

It is the angels and the stars that let people know that Jesus is being born. Heavenly phenomena.

No major media actions, no press conferences, no advertising campaigns. Our Eternal God confides in only a few people, an inconspicuous group of people, who are nevertheless initiated into God's intention with His people. The first witnesses can no longer remain with the old. Their lives are marked by God's Light and God's Love.

Just look at their reactions:
Mary says:

> Here am I, the servant of the Lord; let it be with me according to your word. Luke 1:38

Of her husband Joseph it is said:

> When Joseph awoke from sleep, he did as the angel of the Lord commanded him; he took her as his wife. Matt 1:24

The wise men say to Herod:

> For we observed his star at its rising, and have come to pay him homage. Matt 2:2b

And the shepherds look at each other after the departure of the angels:

> When the angels had left them and gone into heaven, the shepherds said to one another, "Let us go now to Bethlehem and see this thing that has taken place, which the Lord has made known to us." Luke 2:15

Everyone is set in motion towards the child! It is clear that God's entry into our world inspires people to make good resolutions. The new revelation about God's will for people shines like a new light in the lives of those first few chosen ones.

The shepherds give their own wonder as a gift and tell of the words of the angel. Mary stores the words of those simple shepherds well, and she keeps them in her heart and ponders them (Luke 2:19). Then the wise men from their distant countries arrive with maternity gifts at the place where Jesus was born.

The gifts of the wise men

The wise men come from outside the people of Israel. They have to rely on the stars and not on the angels. Yet they bring three significant gifts with them, which are also significant for Israel, namely gold, frankincense, and myrrh.

Israel knows gold from the storage place for the stone tablets of the Ten Commandments, the so-called Ark of the Covenant, which was richly covered with gold.

Gold as a precious and rust-free metal symbolizes the permanent dedication of people to God. After all, you will do anything for your bond with God: it is worth gold!

Frankincense was put in the Temple on the golden sacrificial table "before the face of the Lord," and it was burned on the special altar of incense. Frankincense is an image for the prayers of the faithful: *"Let my prayer be counted as incense before you,"* as it says in the book of Psalms (Psalm 141:2a; cf. Revelation 8:4).

Finally, myrrh is a tree resin, just like frankincense. It not only smells very nice, but also serves as a medicine, a beauty product for women, and an ointment with which the deceased are embalmed. Nicodemus takes myrrh and aloe to anoint Jesus after His death on the cross.

The deeper meaning

What is the deeper meaning of the gifts of the wise men for us? This question can be answered in two ways:

First, the gifts seem to refer very strongly to the death of Jesus. Hadn't the angel told Joseph that this child must be called Jesus because He would save the people from their sins? That has to do with the death of the Lord as an atoning sacrifice. According to the prescriptions of Moses, the incense also has to do with sacrifice. The sacrificed Jesus is anointed with myrrh. In this way, Jesus is initially the sacrificial lamb for his own people Israel. The wise men who come with these three gifts are from outside Israel. They come to do homage. Their arrival indicates that the sacrificial death of Jesus has significance for everyone, even beyond the chosen people of Israel.

Secondly, this broad meaning of Jesus' death indicates that the gifts of the wise men are also given on our behalf. They are, as it were, placed in our hands. You are worth gold if you dedicate your entire life, all your thoughts, actions, and omissions to God. This will only succeed if you remain in contact with God through prayer. May your prayers rise uninterruptedly as incense before God's Face! The Father's expression of love anoints you with myrrh, the oil of the Holy Spirit. The Spirit is a remedy from every evil thought and from all your sins.

Gift for us

We are invited to experience each new year as a gift from God and to give it back as a gift to Him - Who loves us so much.

The good God wants nothing to stand between us and Him that could even slightly obstruct the flow of mutual love.

The more the person can experience God as a gift,
the more he can give his own life to God as a gift
and yet again he will want, together with God,
to give Him as a gift to his fellow human beings!

The King's Children

*High in the sky stands the Star,
The Wise Men come from far,
the Shepherds from close by.
Joseph asks
and his Mary carries
a child,
God's Beloved,
His only Son.
And behold: the Star, which we see in the east,
goes before us
and stands still right above the Child.*

*Be like the Star:
Stand still with the King's Child too!
Yes, you yourself are a King's Child,
for the Newborn will call His Father,*

'Our Father'!

*We all are filled with great joy
At the sight of the Star.
We enter the house of our faith,
we see the Child with His mother Mary
and we pay Him our homage:
We offer the little one, Who is so great,
Our gifts: our hearts,
our devotion,
ourselves!*

*Eight days after His birth
God's Beloved is taken
into the Covenant of God with men.
Then His Name sounds for the first time.
The Name that unites God and men:
'JESUS-GOD SAVES'.*

*God's Message is always a person,
a good Messenger,
a Child, who is a Promise.
On the fortieth day after birth,
the little Jesus
is carried into the Temple in Jerusalem
for the first time.
He is dedicated by his mother and Jozef
to God the Lord.
They have heard,
that a person belongs to God.*

*In the Temple, the old Hannah and Simeon
have been looking forward to see Him for a long time.
Now, monks in the monasteries chant every evening before
going to sleep
the words that Simeon spoke then:*

*Now you may dismiss your servant in peace, O Lord, according to your word.
For my eyes have seen your salvation,*

*which you have prepared before the face of all peoples:
the light of revelation to the nations and the glory of your
people Israel. Luke 2:29-32*

*When Jesus is twelve years old,
He is no longer a child in His Jewish tradition.
He is now a grown man. Three times a year He goes with
His parents
to the Temple in Jerusalem,
to celebrate the three great feasts of
Easter, Pentecost and the Feast of Tabernacles.*

*Now that He has turned twelve, everything is different:
He has become a mature believer,
according to Jewish concepts,
He is now a teacher of Israel.
He is aware that the Temple
is the house of His heavenly Father.
Only there does He really feel at home:
He finds the scholars there,
those who firmly believe,
that where at least two or three of them
are present around the Word of God,
God's Holy Presence
is their true center,
their true Teacher.
That Teacher has now
become their Center as the twelve-year-old Word of God!*

*This is how Jesus' parents find Him
after three days of searching:
He sits among the wise men,
because He Himself is the Word of God:
They all sit around Him.
He is the center,
The conversation is about Him.
Could it be He, the Messiah?
Everyone around Him:
they are full of wonder and admiration.
Yes, He is a wonder to them.*

Jesus goes out into the wide world as the Word of God:
When He speaks in the NAME of the Father,
He speaks words of eternal life,
words that will not perish.
Jesus is the Word that the Father speaks.

He is the Son of the Father.
That is why He will, in the rest of His life,
reflect Himself in the children,
because children are the most obedient
and open to the new.
However, Jesus' disciples have not come to this point yet.
They ask Jesus:

Who is the greatest in the kingdom of heaven? Matt 18:1

You know, the adults
do not want to be children anymore!
Then Jesus calls a child,
Gives it a place in the middle of the circle,
the same Middle where God is,
when people are together in His NAME,
with the One,
then He is Himself, the Word of God.
For He says:

Amen I say to you, unless you change and become like little children, you shall not enter into the kingdom of heaven. Therefore, whoever will have humbled himself like this little child, such a one is greater in the kingdom of heaven. And whoever shall accept one such little child in My name, accepts Me. Luke 18:3-5

Big or small.
It does not matter.
It is better to be
King's children in God's Kingdom together.

For the adults,
Jesus' words are difficult to understand.

*The children are brought to Jesus again and again,
so that Jesus can bless them and pray for them.
But the adults find it too much fuss
and they angrily send away the little ones.
The adults still do not understand Jesus properly.
And Jesus says:*

Allow the little children to come to me, and do not choose to prohibit them. For the kingdom of heaven is among such as these. Matthew 19:14

And to His Father in heaven He prays:

*I acknowledge you, Father, Lord of Heaven and earth, because you have hidden these things from the wise and the prudent, and have revealed them to little ones.
Yes, Father, for this was pleasing before you. Matthew 11: 25-26*

Finally He says to everyone:

*Come to me, all you who labor and have been burdened, and I will refresh you.
Take my yoke upon you, and learn from me, for I am meek and humble of heart; and you shall find rest for your souls. For my yoke is sweet and my burden is light." Matthew 11:28-30*

So is the Kingdom of God in the midst of us, in our hearts!

New Year's Eve news

Do you remember buying your first radio with your hard-earned money? The radio brought the outside world into the living room in a new way. During the war, the radio turned out to be a symbol of hope: listening to Radio Oranje gave courage in fearful days.

And do you also remember how, years later, a television was bought by someone in your neighborhood? Well, that was news! I'm from that era. On Wednesday afternoons, all the children from the neighborhood in The Hague traveled, around the corner on the Laan van Meerdervoort, to watch the children's programs, and for pastries, at the Van Maren house. At Van Maren's, she had seven children, so a few more children didn't really matter in those big mansions. First, we were allowed to go behind the pastry shop at father Van Maren's to pick out a (so-called) 'fallen pastry', and next, we went up the wide stairs where mother Van Maren was waiting for us with a pot of tea. TV on Wednesday afternoon: it was our black-and-white cinema on the street, as in so many cities and villages.

When we didn't yet have a television at home, we sometimes went to the Cineac, the real cinema on the Buitenhof. It was always full of people who came to watch the Polygoon newsreel. And when something important or shocking happened in the world, the cinema was of course very crowded, as full as it could be. I remember the death of Pope John XXIII, who was laid out in St. Peter's, with his mitre on and full attire, fascinating sight. A deceased pope dressed in full regalia. Who would have thought of that? This was my first awareness that people died.

The next modest revolution, while everyone was watching black and white by then, was colour TV. You remember: it went fast at a rapid pace. We could stare at the picture all evening, and then do the same for several days in a row.

The next progress occurred with TV early in the morning. "Who watches television so early?" was my reaction when this was first announced. Apparently that wasn't enough either. We were soon allowed to watch TV 24 hours a day, 7 days a week. Program makers, TV producers, and electronics suppliers apparently assumed that the public had an insatiable hunger for viewing. Thanks to progress, we can now even zap through hundreds of channels worldwide.

Can you no longer keep up with these developments? Don't you watch Netflix, for example? Gosh, you'll miss all the films that have ever been made anywhere in the world. This is correct, because your life is too short to see everything. It's the same with music, because anyone who is even slightly up-to-date spends the whole day streaming their favorite songs. The other day, when my wife and I went to buy a new car, I finally asked about the CD player. My wife looked at me in dismay and asked in astonishment: "Where have you been the past ten years?" The car dealer kept his face businesslike and friendly and confirmed: "Yes, you will get the new system in this car!"

If you ever want to read a good book or a newspaper again… I don't dare to make predictions anymore. I hear from many of you how it used to be. Not everything was perfect then, but it could still be fun to spend time outside with the neighbors. You sang and made music. Every now and then the brass band with fanfare paraded by. "In the past you would sometimes see people standing in groups on the street talking to each other, but not anymore," someone told me.

Now we wonder whether news is still news and whether what is being reported is true. Isn't it fake news, what is presented to us? It seems as if ordinary humanity is wearing out a bit, burdened by all the technical innovations. Fortunately, people are also starting to wonder whether something like artificial intelligence, which is now developing intensively again, will really be progress. Isn't humanity thus perishing from its own success?

How can we rediscover our own humanity? A week without news, newspaper, or anything else? Would that be an idea? Rediscover life, live as you used to do as a child, visit each other and do nice things, tell stories and make music yourself. We have changed with the times. So be it!

Oh well, you still visit each other, fortunately, and….. many other people still do too! All's well that ends well, we might say.

That one day

Regarding the subject of this page, I cannot speak for you but only for myself. This question is valid for you and everyone else.

What will the day be like on which I die? I often wonder. To begin with, on which date will it be? And what age will I have reached on that day? I wish I had the time to give away all my things and especially my books, except for my flute, my glasses, and a Bible. Some time ago I heard the following wonderful story.

Someone told me about her Grandma, a very wise woman, who would be 100 the next day. The whole family had been together, the day before, and was

ready for this birthday. The day was clear and bright.
They all knew that their old mother took her time to get up properly, usually early, because then it was still nice and quiet to be able to pray for a while.

It was eight o' clock, then nine o'clock...That day her prayer had probably been more powerful than in the entire eventful century of her life up to that point. The family slowly began to realize that this day was apparently different.

"I'm going to take a look anyway," said the eldest daughter. Very carefully, she opened slightly the door of her mother's room. Mother was lying very peacefully on the bed, her hands folded with her rosary clasped in them. She was wearing her most beautiful dress and her Sunday hat.

Her face was so beautifully shining and young. It was as if she radiated light. She had got up one more time that morning, early, once and for all!

All her children, grandchildren, and great-grandchildren were now standing around her bed. Their unforgettable mother and grandmother had just turned 100 this time.

On that one grateful day.

*Holy Triune God,
You Who are Love,
and You Who give Love,*

*Grant that we
be Your Love,
O, Holy Triune Love.*

Love as the fullness of life

A prayer to pray continuously, with our unceasing breathing, is a prayer that goes back to the moment of birth. Since our birth, we have been breathing continuously. The unceasing prayer to which the Apostle Paul calls us (1 Thess 5:17) therefore seems an almost divine prayer, because God's breath has been breathed into the human shortly beforehand. Of course, everyone can make his or her own prayer. A few years ago I thought of coming up with a prayer that is completely filled with love.

Holy Triune God

When Jesus was baptized by John the Baptist, something happened that no human being had ever experienced before. The evangelist Mark gives a brief and concise account of it.

> And just as he was coming up out of the water, he saw the heavens torn apart and the Spirit descending like a dove on him. And a voice came from heaven, "You are my Son, the Beloved; with you I am well pleased."
> Mark 1:10-11

What was a confirmation for Jesus gave the bystanders a completely different and new image of God. God exists in community: Father, Son, Spirit, and love is their life.

You Who Are Love

The core message of the entire Bible is: "God is Love." This message cannot be expressed more concisely and powerfully.

And he who abides in love, abides in God, and God in him. This message is given in 1 John 4:16 and Psalm 133:3.

You Who Give Love

A very well-known verse from the Gospel of John is especially loved in the Evangelical Churches:

> For God so loved the world that he gave his only Son, so that everyone who believes in him may not perish but may have eternal life. John 3:16

This is a message about which books have been written. I will limit myself here to just indicating the significance. It is up to you to try to consider it in prayer with uninterrupted breathing. Then you will automatically feel the depth of its significance, but at the same time, the depth of your own heart.

The only goal is to live out this message *with all your heart, with all your soul and with all your strength.* This is the oldest biblical commandment, and Jesus sharpens it with *and love your neighbor as yourself.*

The second part of the prayer is like a mirror, your answer to the first three lines. In this way, prayer is like an infinite circle.

True love has a dynamic from within, it has a transcendent character. Pure love wants to be shared with others, because it is about a shared experience.

The word *experience* already indicates what love is about: it is about life in its totality, intense and joyful. It is being together, living in each other, coming home to each other.

It is like people who, after 60 years of married life, know who the other is as they are completely absorbed in each other, as Jesus says: *Love your neighbor as yourself.*

Grant that we may be Your Love

If we can reach such a height in love, in mutual relationships with other human beings, how much more we will do so when it becomes possible to become one with the Love that is God.

O, Holy Triune Love

The fewer words a prayer contains, the more powerful it is.
Pray in secret, says Jesus.
Where only your Father sees you.
Your own prayer is the most beautiful there is!

Thou

Good God,
Creator since the beginning,
Thou, Who create by calling,
Who call people by their names
and wake them up to service to Thee and fellow human beings.

Early in the morning,
before the dawn,
when all is still with Thy Silence,
and the cock does not yet crow,
and the blackbird does not yet sing,
and the dove does not yet coo,
Thou art the Sun that rises
in the dreams of my heart.
Thou lift me over the heat of the day
by speaking
to the Source of the Living Water,
there Thou say,
while blessing me, to me:

I am he, the one who is speaking to you.[10]
Thou, Father of Jesus and our Father,
Thou, Who takes up thy abode in me,
Who says to me:
I must stay at your house today[11],
Who sanctify and inhabit me as Thy temple,
Who do not flee from my evil thoughts,
from my sinfulness,
but Who only gently
distances Himself when I do not want to see You.
Thou, merciful Father,
Who wait until I would hear Thy Voice,
And understand Thy Word,
Thou, Who see me, Thy prodigal son,
coming from afar,
Who prepare me a banquet,

Thou Who royally clothe my shabbiness,
Who put a ring of bondage on my finger,
when I appreciate Thy grace for me again:
make me listen to Thy Son,

He who says: *Apart from me you can do nothing.*[12]
Who prompts to be obedient and humble:
I did not want to know about it,
of what I have always known and heard
as the Voice of the silent beginning,
as the sound of the Name that is Love.

In the darkness of the night
Thou accompany me as a shining pillar of fire
and during the day as a pillar of cloud,
as once in the desert.

Send me then,
Thou, Who call me to life,

---

10 (John 4:26)

11 Luke 19:5
12 John:15:5

for the sake of my name,
with which Thou called me when I was young,
that this name will protect me
and all those to whom Thou send me
from day to day
from hour to hour counted by you,
raise me up
to Thee, to the One,
the Risen One, the Living One,
My Lord and my God.

AMEN

www.ingramcontent.com/pod-product-compliance
Lightning Source LLC
LaVergne TN
LVHW041709070526
838199LV00045B/1268